POLICY ACTIONS FOR COVID-19 ECONOMIC RECOVERY

A COMPENDIUM OF POLICY BRIEFS

Edited by Ramesh Subramaniam, Alfredo Perdiguero, Jason Rush, and Pamela Asis-Layugan

JUNE 2021

© 2021 Asian Development Bank
6 ADB Avenue, Mandaluyong City, 1550 Metro Manila, Philippines
Tel +63 2 8632 4444; Fax +63 2 8636 2444
www.adb.org

Some rights reserved. Published in 2021.

ISBN 978-92-9262-925-0 (print); 978-92-9262-926-7 (electronic); 978-92-9262-927-4 (ebook)
Publication Stock No. SPR210233-2
DOI: http://dx.doi.org/10.22617/SPR210233-2

The views expressed in this publication are those of the authors and do not necessarily reflect the views and policies of the Asian Development Bank (ADB) or its Board of Governors or the governments they represent.

ADB does not guarantee the accuracy of the data included in this publication and accepts no responsibility for any consequence of their use. The mention of specific companies or products of manufacturers does not imply that they are endorsed or recommended by ADB in preference to others of a similar nature that are not mentioned.

By making any designation of or reference to a particular territory or geographic area, or by using the term "country" in this document, ADB does not intend to make any judgments as to the legal or other status of any territory or area.

Corrigenda to ADB publications may be found at http://www.adb.org/publications/corrigenda.

Notes:
In this publication, "$" refers to United States dollars, unless otherwise stated.
ADB recognizes "China" as the People's Republic of China and "Korea" and "South Korea" as the Republic of Korea.
All photos by ADB unless otherwise indicated.

Cover design by Jordana Queddeng-Cosme.

Contents

Tables and Figures

Tables

Figures

Foreword

The coronavirus disease (COVID-19) has had catastrophic health, social, and economic impacts worldwide. While hope is on the horizon, a multitude of challenges persist.

Collective actions and innovative ideas are required to address this unprecedented crisis. While countries are racing to identify rapid and effective responses to the pandemic, it is also important to lay the groundwork for a future that can better ensure sustainable, inclusive, and resilient growth.

As the COVID-19 pandemic accelerated around the world, the Asian Development Bank (ADB) sponsored the Policy Actions for COVID-19 Economic Recovery (PACER) Dialogues to share cutting-edge knowledge and best practices that could help countries accelerate economic recovery and strengthen cooperation to mitigate the devastating effects of COVID-19.

This compendium of policy briefs from the PACER Dialogues highlights discussions, recommendations, and actionable insights for Southeast Asian countries and the People's Republic of China as they pave the way for post-COVID-19 recovery.

ADB convened the PACER Dialogues from June to September 2020, under the framework of the Brunei Darussalam–Indonesia–Malaysia–Philippines East ASEAN Growth Area (BIMP-EAGA), the Indonesia–Malaysia–Thailand Growth Triangle (IMT-GT), and the Greater Mekong Subregion (GMS) Capacity Building Program, or B-I-G Program.

We hope this compendium will guide policy makers as they traverse multifaceted challenges in the wake of the pandemic and contribute to the crucial work of policy architects, industry players, academics, development practitioners, and other stakeholders as they collaboratively work toward overcoming the worst effects of COVID-19.

Ramesh Subramaniam
Director General, Southeast Asia Department
Asian Development Bank

Abbreviations

ADB	Asian Development Bank
AMC	Advance Market Commitment
ASEAN	Association of Southeast Asian Nations
B-I-G Program	Brunei Darussalam–Indonesia–Malaysia–Philippines East ASEAN Growth Area (BIMP-EAGA), the Indonesia–Malaysia–Thailand Growth Triangle (IMT-GT), and the Greater Mekong Subregion (GMS) Capacity Building Program
BIMP-EAGA	Brunei Darussalam–Indonesia–Malaysia–Philippines East ASEAN Growth Area
CBDC	central bank digital currency
CEPI	Coalition for Epidemic Preparedness Innovations
COVAX	COVID-19 Vaccines Global Access
COVID-19	coronavirus disease
EdTech	education technology
GAVI	Global Alliance for Vaccines and Immunizations
GDP	gross domestic product
GMS	Greater Mekong Subregion
ILO	International Labour Organization
IMT-GT	Indonesia–Malaysia–Thailand Growth Triangle
IOM	International Organization for Migration
MERS-CoV	Middle East respiratory syndrome coronavirus
MSMEs	micro, small, and medium-sized enterprises
PACER	Policy Actions for COVID-19 Economic Recovery
R&D	research and development
Rt	reproductive rate
SARS	severe acute respiratory syndrome
SMEs	small and medium-sized enterprises
UHC	universal health coverage
UNESCO	United Nations Educational, Scientific and Cultural Organization
US	United States
VAT	value-added tax
WHO	World Health Organization
WTTC	World Travel & Tourism Council

Executive Summary

Ramesh Subramaniam
Director General, Southeast Asia Department (SERD), Asian Development Bank (ADB)

Alfredo Perdiguero
Director, Regional Cooperation and Operations Coordination Division, SERD, ADB

Jason Rush
Principal Operations Communications Specialist, SERD, ADB

Pamela Asis-Layugan
Institutional and Capacity Development Specialist (Consultant), SERD, ADB

Chapter 1: Tackling the Impact of COVID-19

Faced with the immense task of protecting both lives and livelihoods, countries need to craft policy responses that can mitigate the economic costs of the coronavirus disease (COVID-19) crisis while minimizing risks to society. **Kwangchul Ji** discusses the "whole of government approach" adopted by the Republic of Korea to protect public health and address the impact of COVID-19, and the successful economic and fiscal measures employed to cushion the economy from the pandemic's fallout and prepare for economic recovery. The Republic of Korea's strategy in tackling COVID-19, widely recognized as an international best practice, has been anchored on transparency and open communication, public–private partnerships, data-driven deployment of public health measures, and innovative solutions hinged on technology and big data.

New Zealand's well-being approach and success in combating COVID-19 also provide valuable lessons. **Mark Blackmore** and **Mario Di Maio** highlight New Zealand's economic response in three waves, guided by the principles of timeliness and fiscal sustainability, targeted to those who need it, and proportionate to the level of the economic shock. The phased approach has helped prevent the spread of COVID-19 while kick-starting recovery and resetting the economy, focusing on trade recovery to sustain supply chains and avoid protectionism.

Small and medium-sized enterprises (SMEs) are considered the backbone of the Asian economy, making up more than 96% of Asian enterprises and contributing 42% of gross domestic product (GDP). In the Association of Southeast Asian Nations (ASEAN), SMEs provide 50% of employment. An ADB survey conducted in four ASEAN economies found that more than half of micro, small, and medium-sized enterprises (MSMEs) were facing severe shortages of working capital and inadequate access to formal financial services in the wake of the pandemic, raising concerns about debt service capacity and business sustainability. With rapid and sharp declines in demand, disruptions in economic activities, and a surge in job losses worldwide, many SMEs are at risk and bear the brunt of the economic crisis.

Paul Vandenberg discusses measures to help SMEs respond to and begin recovering from the crisis, including tax deferment, credit, wage subsidies, enterprise pivots, and policy advice to weather the crisis.

Chapter 2: Protecting the Poor and Vulnerable

Global evidence illustrates that pandemics' burden falls disproportionately on poor and marginalized populations, including migrants and their families. The migrant workforce is particularly vulnerable to the economic slowdown resulting from the COVID-19 pandemic.

As countries act to tackle the crisis, a strong case can be made for an inclusive public health and socioeconomic response to control the virus, restart economies, and stay on track to achieve the Sustainable Development Goals. Migrant-inclusive approaches with universal health coverage as a goal are crucial not only for overcoming the threats posed by COVID-19, but also for protecting public health at a lower overall cost, leading to improved development outcomes. **Patrick Duigan** proposes a three-track policy agenda to address the complex challenges of COVID-19 to migrant health and immigration. The policy agenda aims to reduce transmission risks, mitigate impacts, and leverage opportunities for transformational changes in managing human mobility and migration.

Valentina Barca and **Edward Archibald** highlight that COVID-19 necessitates the adoption of social protection systems and the rapid scale-up of social assistance to address the pandemic's impacts. While countries' ability to provide social protection to their populations is largely determined by the strength of their social protection systems before COVID-19, countries can still modify and ensure the sustainability of these systems during and beyond the pandemic. Shock-responsive policy design needs to consider the three dimensions of adequacy, coverage, and comprehensiveness in existing or new social protection programs.

Chapter 3: Accelerating Digital Transformation

Digital technologies are necessary for managing the COVID-19 crisis and unlocking the full potential of the digital economy. Digital platforms are proving to be critical in reshaping the way we live and create economic value in a post-pandemic world. With the "cash-light economy" emerging as a key tool in surviving the COVID-19 and similar future outbreaks, the crisis reinforces the importance of digital infrastructure as a key enabler to leapfrogging technological advancements, especially for the financial sector. **David Lee Kuo Chuen** discusses policies that can help accelerate the growth of digital financial services, digital payment infrastructures, and open-banking platforms during and after the COVID-19 pandemic.

Arndt Husar argues that the post-COVID-19 new normal calls for supporting start-up ecosystems with increasing returns to scale due to network effects. An increase in the number of start-ups in the ecosystem leads to the community's growth behind the ecosystem—such as capital, talent, universities, and support organizations—which, in turn, produces more value. Saving start-ups can help transition the wider economy to a new normal and put it on the path to digital transformation.

On the education front, the COVID-19 pandemic has aggravated the existing learning crisis, especially for low-income and middle-income countries, with an estimated 1.5 billion students out of school in 165 countries, leading to greater losses in lifetime opportunities and earnings. Before the COVID-19 outbreak, physical access was not an issue, but with the ensuing crisis, access and learning quality are now key contributing factors to realizing effective literacy and numeracy skills of school children. Massive school closures have led to increased interest in distance learning and using education technology (EdTech) solutions, or the use of technology and digital innovations to improve learning and teaching. A sudden increase in online learning provides opportunities to reimagine education in post-pandemic situations.

Ashish Dhawan promotes an equity-focused digital strategy for education, drawing from India's experience in improving the quality of school and higher education through evidence and innovation-driven reforms, and using EdTech solutions for learning and employability. **Chad Pasha** features lessons on mitigating education disruptions and job losses based on Coursera's Campus Response and Workforce Recovery Initiatives.

Chapter 4: Reigniting Southeast Asia and Bouncing Back Stronger Together

This final chapter examines how economies in lockdown can best restart during and after the COVID-19 pandemic, and what can be done to revitalize the hard-hit tourism sector. It also highlights regional cooperation responses to complement national strategies, emphasizing regional public goods in health and tourism.

Early in the COVID-19 crisis, policy makers used various measures to mitigate the spread of the pandemic. Many countries imposed several forms of lockdowns, with varying stages of unlocking or easing containment measures. Epidemic control measures come with attendant societal and economic costs. Countries are still grappling with the issues: what minimum package of measures should be retained, what measures can be relaxed, and what optimal sequence can pave the way for cautious economic reopening.

Jeremy Lim suggests a stepladder approach in four levels for a post-lockdown period based on resource availability, with a caveat that there is no single optimal formula. He notes careful consideration is needed based on the country's capacity and infrastructure. The stepladder approach underscores epidemic control measures built around key points in the virus' transmission pathways, including border controls, active measures to identify and isolate cases and close contacts, and general community and mitigation measures.

Anup Malani showcases adaptive control as a flexible countercyclical policy approach, whereby different areas are released from lockdown in potentially different gradual ways depending on the local progression of the disease. Adaptive control as applied in suppression policies and forecasting for vaccination policies is elaborated with corresponding policy outcomes.

Immunization is an important global public health good and holds the potential for providing a cost-effective way of ultimately protecting people from COVID-19. As vaccines become more available, countries face challenges of guaranteeing equitable access to vaccines and ensuring that health-care workers and those most at risk are prioritized. A strategy for phased vaccine rollout and continued pandemic control using public health measures and other tools needs to be guided by international cooperation. **Farzana Muhib**, **Hannah Kettler**, and **Huong Vu Minh** outline global financing options, demand scenarios, and other measures countries should consider in preparing for safe, effective, and equitable vaccine delivery amid COVID-19.

Despite tourism's proven resilience to past crises, the worldwide depth and breadth of the COVID-19 pandemic will likely continue to dampen travel and tourism demand in the medium term and have a longer-lasting effect on international tourism until effective prevention and treatment measures are widely available. The pause in tourism activity caused by COVID-19 provides governments and the travel and tourism stakeholders with an exceptional opportunity to strengthen and accelerate measures to ensure the sector is sustainable, inclusive, and resilient. **Tiffany Misrahi** elaborates steps to help the tourism industry recover in the wake of the pandemic, including phased approaches to mitigate impact, restart the travel and tourism sector, reach recovery, and redesign tourism for the new normal.

CHAPTER 1
Tackling the Impact of COVID-19

Policy Lessons from a Pandemic: The Korean Experience

Kwangchul Ji
Director of International Financial Institutions Division
Ministry of Economy and Finance, Republic of Korea

COVID-19 testing. A drive-through screening center in Incheon collects specimens for COVID-19 diagnostic testing (photo by iStock/Goldcastle7).

Introduction

When the World Health Organization (WHO) officially declared the coronavirus disease (COVID-19) outbreak as a pandemic on 11 March 2020, the Republic of Korea was already reporting more patient recoveries than new cases. The country responded quickly and undertook several policy measures to "flatten the curve" and reduce the number of new cases daily. As the health crisis threatened to infect its real economy as well, the Republic of Korea implemented a more coordinated approach at the local, national, and international levels to cushion its economy and its people from the COVID-19 fallout and took these extraordinary measures:

1. The Government of the Republic of Korea focused its capacity and resources on containing the spread of the virus through a three-pronged strategy of Test, Trace, and Treat (3Ts).

2. It adopted fiscal and monetary policies to boost the economy and domestic consumption, support vulnerable sectors, and protect markets from external shocks.

3. It set its priorities clearly—from identifying COVID-19 patients who needed immediate treatment to assisting vulnerable individuals and distressed businesses. The government also provided industry-specific support to its most vital industries as well as to microbusiness owners and the self-employed.

Context

On 19 January 2020, the Republic of Korea announced its first confirmed COVID-19 case. The government immediately recognized the need for prompt and comprehensive action and swiftly responded by conducting large-scale testing.

Its quick response shows how the Republic of Korea has learned its lesson from previous health crises such as the severe acute respiratory syndrome (SARS) epidemic in 2004 and the Middle East respiratory syndrome coronavirus (MERS-CoV) outbreak in 2015. Since then, the country has strengthened its capacity for disease control, including training public health staff at the national and local levels on contact tracing and epidemiological investigation, enabling the government to rapidly deploy testing stations and trace and treat patients during the outbreak.

The Republic of Korea also relied on its modern and affordable health-care system and public adherence to national health advice such as wearing face masks and social distancing. Its digital infrastructure also came in handy for contact tracing, health diagnosis, and information dissemination.

Strong cooperation between the public and private sectors played a huge role in the country's COVID-19 response. The government swiftly eased regulations so private medical companies can produce and distribute test kits faster to meet the growing demand. As early as January 2020, with only four confirmed cases, test kits were already developed in the country; by March, they were being exported to 81 countries.

As soon as the government raised its crisis alert level to the highest (Level 4) on 23 February 2020, it immediately assembled the Central Disaster and Safety Countermeasure Headquarters, headed by no less than the Prime Minister, to set priorities and coordinate policy responses at the local, national, and international levels. Policies are immediately cascaded down to the local governments to ensure the adequacy of hospitals and beds for patients. If the cases are beyond the capacity of local governments, the central government provides the necessary resources. This clear delineation of responsibilities led to rapid response and policy actions.

Policy Implementation

For the Republic of Korea, early detection is key to preventing the virus from spreading. Its 3Ts strategy is done through these measures:

- **Special entry procedures.** The government adopted special entry procedures that required all inbound travelers, including Korean nationals, to undergo a 14-day self-quarantine or isolation, a body temperature check, and other measures. A self-quarantine safety protection app or self-diagnosis app was made available for people to monitor and report symptoms of infection during their stay in the country from their mobile phones. Each local government (city or province) is provided with a list of inbound passengers for closer monitoring.

- **Screening and testing stations.** To easily detect infected patients, the government made diagnostic test facilities widely available. Aside from screening clinics at public health centers and health-care institutions, it rolled out testing facilities, drive-through centers, mobile facilities, and door-to-door visits for specimen collections. Travelers can also get tested in walk-through facilities at Incheon International Airport and get their sample collected in 5 minutes or less.

- **Contact tracing.** The central and local governments conducted prompt epidemiological investigation and quarantine of contacts. In addition to obtaining basic information on the confirmed patients' whereabouts and interviewing health-care workers and family members, the government also gathered data from medical records, mobile GPS, CCTV footage, and credit card records. Medical institutions also had access to patients' overseas travel history.

- **Patient management system.** The order of treatment of confirmed COVID-19 patients is based on the severity of their cases. To ensure the availability of medical facilities for non-COVID-19 patients, the government designated COVID-19 protection hospitals. It also allowed nonrespiratory patients to receive medical advice and prescriptions by phone to avoid exposure to the virus.

To cushion the pandemic's economic fallout, the government adopted fiscal policies to

- protect jobs, vulnerable groups, and businesses;
- promote consumption and industries; and
- prepare for the shift to the "new normal" with new business regulations and the "Korean New Deal."

To protect the economy

- Four financial stimulus packages and other emergency relief, amounting to $210 billion or equivalent to 13% of the country's GDP, were released. These will fund programs designed to help businesses survive, ease borrowers' payment burden, avoid a credit crunch, among others.

- A historically high supplementary budget of W11.7 trillion ($10 billion) was passed by the National Assembly to aid in disease prevention and treatment, small business loans, household support (including day care vouchers), livelihood support, and relief for hard-hit sectors.

To promote economic recovery

- Industry-specific emergency financing is given to four vital industries: airlines, shipping, tourism, and the arts.

- Incentives are provided to entice domestic consumption, such as extending emergency relief to all households; doubling income tax deduction for credit or debit card use; expanding local governments' gift certificates issuance; and issuing leisure and tourism coupons, as well as maternal health-care coupons.

To prepare for economic recovery

- The government will improve business regulations in 10 sectors that will be highly in demand in the new normal: big data or artificial intelligence, future cars mobility, health care, financial technology (fintech), medical technologies, recycling, venture start-ups, industrial complexes, tourism, and e-commerce. Remote health care and education and online businesses will also be a focus.

- The government unveiled the Korean New Deal, a W76 trillion ($62 billion) spending plan to establish a digital infrastructure and create new jobs to prepare the economy for the new normal.

Complementing these fiscal measures were the following monetary policies:

- Reduce interest rates.
- Raise the trading limit on foreign exchange futures to prevent sudden volatility in the swap market.
- Engage in a bilateral currency swap with the United States Federal Reserve.
- Ensure an unlimited supply of liquidity to Korean financial institutions.
- Extend financing for special purpose vehicles to purchase corporate bonds and other market stabilization measures.

Policy Outcomes

On 29 February 2020, the Republic of Korea recorded the highest number of COVID-19 patients of any country outside the People's Republic of China—909 cases—mainly due to a religious gathering in Daegu City. By the end of March 2020, however, the number of new cases dropped to 78.

The country of over 50 million managed to bring down the number of cases dramatically in just a month without resorting to restricting movement or shutting down borders. It took immediate recognition of the problem from the top; clear-cut and decisive policy actions; close cooperation with local and national authorities; sharing of vital information; and preemptive, bold, and sufficient steps to revive the economy beyond the COVID-19 pandemic.

Lessons

The Republic of Korea's COVID-19 response offers lessons for countries facing similar challenges:

1. **Act swiftly and decisively.** When the pandemic started, the government did not have a budget for its COVID-19 response as its budget priorities were already in place. To fund its response and the economic relief and fiscal stimulus package to assist the economy's vulnerable sectors, the government used two supplemental budgets and its reserve fund. It also asked the National Assembly for a special budget approval procedure and a third supplemental budget. The government used all its available fiscal resources to come up with quick solutions and "extinguish the fire," preventing the problem from festering. While it had some successes, not all its fiscal policies worked, but it was flexible and open to policy changes to achieve its objectives.

2. **Be transparent to earn public trust.** From the beginning, the government ensured there is transparency in the process by sharing its crisis response policies and the purpose of the diagnostic tests. This transparency led to a greater public understanding of the government's actions and prevented chaos and anxiety over the mass testing.

3. **Set the tone from the top.** While the central government acted swiftly toward the pandemic, the local governments also played an important role, particularly in the contact tracing. Local governments formed an emergency committee that was chaired by no less than the Prime Minister, who attended the daily meetings, sending a signal that the policy decisions directly emanate from the top and ensuring they are acted upon quickly.

4. **Conduct mass testing.** The government shouldered all the costs of mass testing to the tune of $76 million, regardless of whether the person is a Korean national or a foreigner. Mass testing eliminated the stigma toward COVID-19 patients as everyone has to undergo testing.

5. **Gather multisector support.** Enjoin various sectors to cooperate and help in the government's response. When there was a shortage of face masks at the onset, the public and private companies in the Republic of Korea gave financial support and mobilized their own supply chain networks in making the face masks. They also offered their facilities as treatment centers. Individual citizens lent their support by abiding by the rules on social distancing, wearing masks, and nonparticipation in mass gatherings such as religious worship. Landlords also voluntarily reduced the rent of small businesses to help them cope with the pandemic's economic fallout.

6. **Build on past lessons.** Even before COVID-19, Korean citizens were already accustomed to wearing face masks because of SARS and MERS-CoV experiences. Dealing with these previous health crises also built up the country's manufacturing facilities, which enabled it to produce masks at the rate of almost 10 million a day.

7. **Balance public health and economic growth.** While protecting the health of its people, the government must also support the economy. Being a major semiconductor exporter, the Republic of Korea relies heavily on the interconnectedness of global trade, so the government needs to help companies manage the disruption in their supply chain and reconnect to the global value chain. The government did it through bilateral negotiations, cooperation, and dialogues with other countries to grant special entry for emergencies or for professionals in critical industries. The government also helped provide health certifications to assure its trading partners that the Korean workers traveling to their countries were virus-free.

8. **Protect the vulnerable sectors.** At the onset, the Republic of Korea was not prepared to provide financial support for informal or casual workers. The government, however, is extending financial support such as an employment insurance fund to help vulnerable sectors, including artists and freelancers not covered by the fund. While the current funding may not be enough to help all vulnerable sectors survive the pandemic, the government said it is open to fine-tuning its policies.

Resources

Kwangchul Ji, Ministry of Economy and Finance, Republic of Korea. 2020. Republic of Korea's Policy Experience in Responding to COVID-1. Presented at ADB's PACER Dialogues. 3 June.

Ministry of Economy and Finance. Tackling COVID-19 in South Korea. 16 April 2020. YouTube video, 4:29.

Lessons We Can Learn from New Zealand's COVID-19 Strategy

Mark Blackmore
Senior Representative for Singapore, India, and Southeast Asia New Zealand Treasury

Mario Di Maio
Principal Advisor, New Zealand Treasury

Social distancing. After more than 2 weeks of no active cases, New Zealand lifted restrictions on gatherings and domestic travel in June 2020 and no longer required, but still encouraged social distancing (photo by iStock/Lakeview Images).

Introduction

When the coronavirus disease (COVID-19) arrived in late February 2020 in New Zealand, its government quickly responded with tough measures: rapid mass testing, robust contact tracing, border closures, full lockdown, and a 14-day self-quarantine for those coming home to the country. The goal is to be "virus-free" after recording more than 1,000 confirmed cases in March 2020.

New Zealand has since been seeing a steady decline in the number of new cases. By 8 June 2020, its four-tiered alert system was brought down to level 1, the lowest level, after no new cases were reported for more than 2 weeks. Its relative success with its "go hard, go early" strategy in handling the health crisis has drawn global attention.

While it has managed to flatten the curve early, the Government of New Zealand now faces the daunting task of jump-starting its economy. It has put in place a broad range of initiatives to kick-start economic activity, create decent and sustainable jobs, ensure the security of the most vulnerable, and lay the groundwork for long-term recovery. Among the nonfiscal policy measures deemed critical to recovery is its trade recovery strategy.

Some Inherent Advantages

In tackling the health crisis, New Zealand has some distinct advantages:

1. **Geography.** New Zealand is a remote island nation, and few flights transit through it. It can easily seal borders and control the entry of people.
2. **Size.** It has a sparse population of 5 million. Fewer people encounter each other, so the virus cannot spread as easily.
3. **Governance.** The country is centrally governed and does not have states, making it easier to enforce policies.

Yet, the government still saw it fit to take a preemptive approach—go hard, go early—to stop the spread of the virus. One reason it took strong action is its role as the gateway or key departure route to the Pacific island countries. It needs to protect its Pacific neighbors from the pandemic, which also favors its people.

Some of the stringent measures, however, had a significant impact on its economy. The country's strict border restrictions adversely affected the tourism industry, while the domestic lockdown saw most industries and services temporarily halted.

In the same way it tackled the health crisis, the government acted swiftly in cushioning the economic impacts, which have caused great uncertainty. New Zealand entered the crisis with a robust macroeconomy and a healthy fiscal position with low debt levels, enabling the government to fund its massive economic and fiscal stimulus packages.

Go Hard, Go Early

While New Zealand enjoys inherent advantages, such as being an island nation, its formula in dealing with the health crisis is replicable:

1. **Swift and decisive action.** The country had five confirmed cases only when COVID-19 was officially declared a global pandemic. It nonetheless responded fast by closing its borders to foreign travelers and enforcing a 14-day home quarantine for those coming home. Ten days later, it introduced full lockdown measures, among the strictest by international standards.
2. **Massive testing.** New Zealand ramped up testing to the point that it can now carry out up to 8,000 tests per day—one of the highest rates per capita in the world. It also strengthened its contact tracing capability, including using a COVID-19 tracer app that requires users to create a digital diary of their whereabouts.

3. **Effective communication.** Keeping citizens informed is a critical element of the COVID-19 response. One example is the four-level COVID-19 Alert System that assesses the risk level from infection and gets updated based on available scientific data and intervention measures. Daily press conferences featuring the Prime Minister and the Director-General of Health were also held.

Economic Response in Three Waves

New Zealand's economic response is guided by three principles: timely and fiscally sustainable, targeted to those who need it, and proportionate to the level of the economic shock. The responses are in three waves:

1. Wave One: Fighting the Virus, Cushioning the Blow
2. Wave Two: Kick-Starting the Recovery
3. Wave Three: Resetting and Rebuilding the Economy

To inform its economic policy advice to the government, the New Zealand Treasury considers the potential impact on the multidimensional well-being of citizens. It is also taking a long-term view—how the COVID-19 pandemic will alter New Zealanders' future well-being.

The Treasury uses the Living Standards Framework Dashboard shown in Figure 1.1, which provides indicators of current well-being across 12 domains (e.g., health, housing, safety, and social connections) and around future well-being framed by natural capital, human capital, social capital, and financial and physical capital. The indicators are internationally comparable where possible, while reflecting some of what is unique about New Zealand and New Zealanders. The data show New Zealanders' current and future well-being, broken down by ethnicity, age, gender, region, family type, and area deprivation over time. The data also show the distribution of high, medium, and low well-being for each domain.

Wave One: Fighting the Virus and Cushioning the Blow

These measures were implemented swiftly to help various sectors, including the vulnerable ones to cope with the immediate negative economic impacts of COVID-19. The government coordinated with the financial and business sectors for support.

Economic Response Package

The initial NZ$12.1 billion ($8 billion)—approximately 7%–8% of New Zealand's gross domestic product (GDP)—is meant to protect citizens' health and well-being, safeguard livelihoods, and ensure the quickest recovery on all fronts.

Figure 1.1: The Treasury's Living Standards Framework

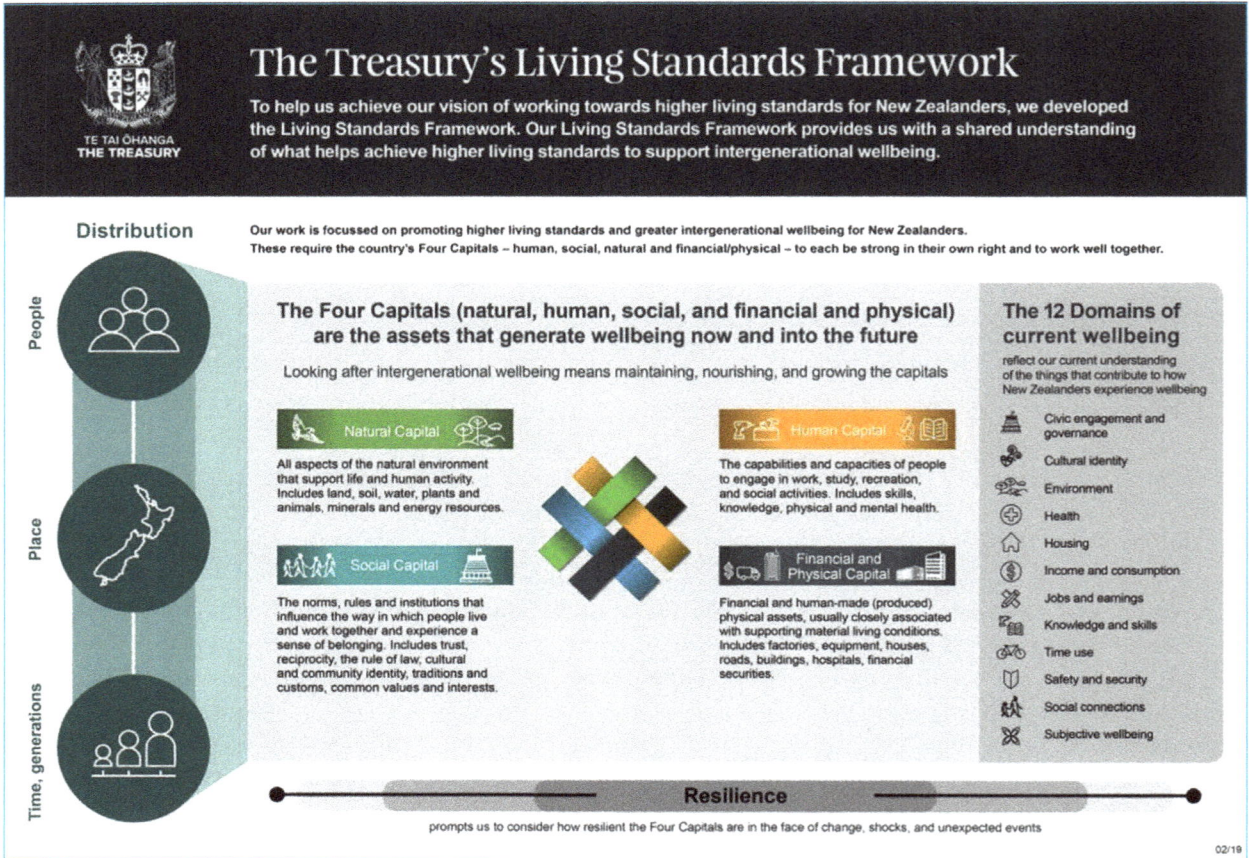

Source: New Zealand Treasury.

COVID-19 Response and Recovery Fund

Amounting to NZ$50 billion ($32 billion), this serves as supplementary funding for the Economic Response Package measures.

Monetary Policy Support

The Reserve Bank of New Zealand launched various monetary, fiscal, and financial measures to shore up liquidity and ensure cash flow among banks, firms, households, and the government. Measures also aimed to keep the financial system stable, ensuring that foreign exchange and debt and money markets are operating efficiently and at low cost.

Business Finance Guarantee

This scheme would enable banks to provide loans to businesses.

Wage Subsidy

A quick-response package of more than NZ$10 billion ($6.56 billion) was provided to support employers, employees, and the self-employed.

Small Business Cash Flow (Loans)

This immediate cash flow support, amounting to NZ$5 billion ($3.28 billion), aims to address the risk of widespread business failures among small and medium-sized enterprises (SMEs).

Household Support Measures

These are measures to ease the financial burden of households.

Wave Two: Kick-Starting the Recovery

These are measures to aid economic recovery, including exit from extraordinary measures adopted when the risk to COVID-19 was still high. These measures are expected to last for 12–18 months.

Wave 3: Resetting and Rebuilding the Economy

These are measures to address long-standing challenges to ensure a sustainable fiscal and economic position in New Zealand.

Trade Recovery Strategy

Because of the uncertainties brought about by the COVID-19 crisis and to reinforce international cooperation, the government adjusted its overall approach to trade policy and launched a trade recovery strategy on 8 June 2020. The goal is three-pronged: support exporters, reinvigorate trade, and renew key trade relationships. The government engaged in bilateral agreements to facilitate trade and essential cross-border travel while still safeguarding public health. These initiatives helped lay the foundation for the country's short- to medium-term trade recovery strategy.

Outcomes

As a result of the health and economic response measures,

- New Zealand has one of the lowest cases of COVID-19 per capita in the world.[1]

- Daily life and activities in the country have essentially gone back to pre-COVID-19 norms, and its alert level is back to its lowest as the risk of infection dissipates.

- While New Zealand's border remains essentially closed, the government has taken bilateral measures to keep trade flowing for goods critical to its COVID-19 response, such as importing personal protective equipment and medicine. It is also exploring ways to rebuild confidence in travel and tourism, also a major contributor to its economy apart from trade.

- Extreme uncertainty remains as the country anticipates the pandemic's economic cost to be substantial and the impact longer-lasting.

The Treasury expects the pandemic to alter the well-being of future generations of New Zealanders, particularly in four areas: natural capital (i.e., impact on the environment); financial and physical capital (i.e., loss of wealth and decline in financial assets); human capital (i.e., disruption to learning, a decline in skills and life expectancy); and social capital (i.e., limited access to public services, feeling of isolation and discrimination).

Lessons

New Zealand's COVID-19 response offers lessons for countries facing similar challenges:

Data and science must inform the government in its policy decisions and actions. New Zealand used scientific data to establish a level of certainty that the measures it will take will not result in an increase in COVID-19 cases and force it to reverse track and reestablish hard lockdown measures. The Treasury uses a multidimensional well-being approach to gauge the impact of its policy responses on New Zealanders' current and future well-being. The impact is tracked by the Living Standards Framework Dashboard, first launched in December 2018.

Speed, simplicity, and effectiveness of the measures are important. The government deemed it essential to move quickly to cushion the pandemic's blows, particularly to vulnerable sectors. An example is the Wage Subsidy Scheme meant to support those who have lost their jobs because of COVID-19. While the scheme is expensive for the government (more than NZ$15 billion or nearly $10 billion), it was simple to implement and effective (1.6 million jobs saved in the first phase). As New Zealand was on a high-alert level for a short time, the scheme lasted only 12 weeks. The government shifted to an exit strategy by tightening the eligibility of firms. Other measures are the Small Business Cashflow Scheme and Income Relief Payment, which protect small businesses.

---

[1]   Worldometers.info. COVID-19 Coronavirus Pandemic. https://www.worldometers.info/coronavirus/ (accessed 15 July 2020).

Agility is important in government. The crisis has changed the government's short- to medium-term priorities. To manage the external shocks and mitigate the economic impact on New Zealanders' well-being, which it views as a more important indicator than GDP, the government acted fast in realigning its budget priorities; recalibrating policy measures such as health spending, benefits payments, and education; and resetting targets. Its healthy fiscal position and favorable credit rating enabled the government to fund COVID-19 response measures by issuing bonds: $3.5 billion in April 2020 and $7.0 billion in June 2020.

Protect the most vulnerable sectors immediately and adjust to the needs accordingly. The government identified the economy's most vulnerable sectors and responded with an initial financial stimulus package that it expanded as the need arose. One example is NZ$1.5 billion ($1.09 billion) in loans for SMEs with fewer than five employees. The government announced the extension of the loans to SMEs till December 2020. The amount has not increased, and there is no discussion on further extension at this stage.

Keep trade open even with borders closed. New Zealand is heavily reliant on trade and tourism, but it had to seal off its borders and control foreigners' entry to contain the spread of the virus. Now that it is slowly relaxing its border restrictions, the government has engaged its counterparts around the region to keep connections open and place specific measures for aviation. These include temporary assistance to airlines; bilateral engagements on flights; and "travel bubbles," which allow people to hop off on planes without requiring self-quarantine. It also mounted initiatives to sustain trade and supply chain connectivity and to avoid protectionism measures. Earlier initiatives include the New Zealand–Singapore Air Freight Project and the bilateral agreement on trade in essential goods with Singapore, as well as the signing of ministerial statements.

Resources

M. Blackmore and M. Di Maio. 2020. COVID-19: A Summary of New Zealand Policy Response So Far. Presented at ADB's PACER Dialogues. 17 June.

Government of New Zealand. 2020. *Budget 2020: Rebuilding Together*. Feature. 14 May.

_____. 2020. COVID-19 Economic Response Package. Feature. 15 April.

Government of New Zealand, Ministry of Health. COVID-19.

Government of New Zealand, The Treasury. COVID-19 Economic Package at a Glance.

_____. 2020. COVID-19 Income Relief Payment Announced. News. 25 May.

_____. 2020. *He Kāhui Waiora: Living Standards Framework and He Ara Waiora COVID-19: Impacts on Wellbeing (DP 20/02)*. Discussion Paper. 9 July.

_____. 2020. Summary of Initiatives in the COVID-19 Response and Recovery Fund (CRRF) Foundational Package. 29 May.

_____. 2020. Support for Businesses Affected by COVID-19 Extended. News. 5 June.

Government of New Zealand. Unite against COVID-19.

H. D. Parker. 2020. Trade Strategy for the Recovery from the Impacts of Covid-19. Speech. 8 June. Government of New Zealand.

Reserve Bank of New Zealand. COVID-19.

How Small and Medium-Sized Enterprises Can Bounce Back from the COVID-19 Crisis

Paul Vandenberg
Senior Economist, Economic Research and Regional Cooperation Department
Asian Development Bank

Missing customers. Shops and restaurants are open for business, but customers are few and far between in this once-bustling district in Singapore.

Introduction

Small and medium-sized enterprises (SMEs), considered the backbone of many economies, have been badly hurt by the coronavirus disease (COVID-19) pandemic. Transport and border restrictions, social distancing, and lockdowns have disrupted supply chains, dampened consumer demand, and shrank cash flow. As a result, small businesses cannot pay store rent, workers' wages, suppliers, and creditors, creating a spiraling effect on households and the economy.

Governments are now grappling with policies to support SMEs, which collectively employ an average of 60% of Asia's workforce. In addition to general macroeconomic policies, a "bounce back" strategy that looks at the enterprise level is needed to help SMEs survive the pandemic and in the new business environment that will emerge afterward.

SMEs can also benefit from policies that promote the flow of goods and services within and across borders and that support their increased participation in regional and global supply chains.

Five Challenges

The world is now facing unprecedented challenges from COVID-19. What initially started as a health emergency has rapidly evolved into one of the worst economic crises in history. For many SMEs, the challenge is to hurdle not just one but a series of crises—health, economics, and business—with stages that largely depend on the speed by which the government can contain the spread of the virus and jump-start the economy.

The first pan-Asian survey on the impact of COVID-19 on SMEs in the region, conducted by the Asia Pacific MSME Trade Coalition from 31 March to 6 April 2020, revealed that the pandemic's impact on small businesses has been immediate. According to the survey, these are the five major challenges that face SMEs (Figure 1.2):

1. Lack of operational cash flow (almost 50% of SMEs surveyed have less than a month or just a month of cash reserves)

2. Low customer demand

3. Business closure due to state lockdown policies

4. Reduced opportunities to meet new clients

5. Issues that entail changing business models and strategies and providing new products or services

Figure 1.2: Key Challenges for Micro, Small, and Medium-Sized Enterprises

1 Lack of operational cash flow

2 Drop in demand for products and services

3 CLOSED — Business is closed

4 Reduction of opportunities to meet new clients

5 Issues with changing business strategies to offer alternative products and services

MSMEs also find difficulties obtaining raw materials, providing logistics and shipping of products. Workers are also not able to return to work.

MSMEs = micro, small, and medium-sized enterprises.
Source: Asia Pacific MSME Trade Coalition. 2020. COVID-19 SME Impact Survey.

Unless these issues are addressed through government policy interventions and other initiatives, many SMEs are in danger of closure. As it is, according to the Asia Pacific MSME Trade Coalition, nearly one-third of SMEs expect to lay off 50% or more of their workers to survive.

Mitigation and Recovery Measures

Governments have started to put in place a wide array of measures to mitigate the economic impact of the COVID-19 outbreak on businesses. Some have focused on more general policies intended to cushion the blow for the economy and all businesses.

Many countries are also deploying a wide range of policy instruments to support SMEs and particularly the self-employed during this extremely difficult time. The immediate focus is addressing short-term liquidity. Such policies take various shapes, and here are some of the most common:

- **Tax deferment.** Income taxes, property taxes, excise duties, and other payments remitted by businesses to the government are deferred to ease SMEs' liquidity constraints.
- **Credit.** The government increases credit availability to SMEs using several approaches: direct lending through state-owned banks, reducing interest rates on special loan programs or relaxing monetary policy by the central bank, expanding the use of credit guarantee schemes, or extending grace periods on existing loans.
- **Wage subsidy.** The government partially covers the cost of enterprises in providing wage and income support for employees laid off temporarily, or in safeguarding employment.
- **Enterprise pivot.** The government encourages SMEs to adapt to the emerging business environment by pivoting or shifting to another business model or other products and services.

In addition, the government can also advise on how SMEs can weather the pandemic, manage their cash flow and their workforce, and provide other information that can guide them on the road to recovery.

Policy Implications

The pandemic's economic impact on small businesses varies greatly, mainly depending on the speed of government response to the spread of the virus. As such, policy makers need to consider and weigh the implications of the policy instruments they plan to deploy.

Here are some of the pros and cons of each policy instrument:

Tax Deferment

Pros: The COVID-19 crisis struck just when businesses were due to pay their taxes in the second quarter of 2020. The tax deferrals by the government (usually by 3–6 months) during the lockdown period helped ease the pressure on cash flow.

Cons: As businesses were unable to operate during the lockdown period, they had less profit and thus had less tax payments to make. This adds fiscal pressure on the government and consequently reduces its ability to fund more relief and recovery programs for the sector and the economy as a whole. It also lessens its ability to extend tax deferments or other concessions to assist businesses further.

Credit

Pros: Extending direct credit, credit guarantees, or a grace period on debt payment enables SMEs to obtain working capital so they can stay in operation and pay wages.

Cons: Fresh credit incurred or deferred payment still have to be paid, potentially causing difficulty for the SMEs to repay the credit even if moved to a later date. This increases the risk of having nonperforming loans, causing instability in banks and the financial system.

Pros: Lower interest rates on borrowings reduce the cost of credit for SMEs and ease their liquidity position.

Cons: Reducing interest rates may not effectively stimulate the economy if interest rates are already low. It might also just keep insolvent firms temporarily afloat.

Pros: Extending a government credit guarantee encourages private lenders to assist SMEs, as this reduces their credit risk.

Cons: Enabling commercial banks to disburse the government loan subsidy may not be effective, as banks tend to favor larger firms as less risky and view the transaction only from a profitability angle. The government needs to replenish the credit guarantee fund to sustain the scheme. It takes time to develop an effective credit guarantee scheme.

Wage Subsidy

Pros: A government wage subsidy helps SMEs keep their workers employed and earning wages. This, in turn, serves as social protection, as it eases the pressure on other types of social assistance.

Cons: A wage subsidy is costly, requiring a large financial outlay for the government, which effectively becomes the "private sector's salary paymaster." Some countries are not prepared to administer the subsidy, causing bureaucratic bottlenecks and delays in releasing the payout. The scheme is also not easy to administer in the case of enterprises in the informal sector.

Enterprise Pivot

Pros: The lockdowns have shown the government and SMEs the importance of pursuing the e-commerce agenda and digital technology, particularly in digital finance, online sales and delivery, and customer service. The pandemic has also put to the test the agility of SMEs to change their business model, with some immediately redirecting their production to needed products (e.g., masks, personal protective equipment, ventilators).

Cons: Some countries are not ready to pivot to digital due to poor connectivity and low investment in information and communication technology.

Policy Implementation

It may still be too early to assess the effectiveness of the policy instruments that some countries have adopted as part of their bounce-back strategy to assist SMEs. However, here are some examples of how countries have implemented them:

Tax Deferment

- **People's Republic of China.** Extension of the deadline for filing tax returns; lower value-added tax (VAT) on medical services, catering and accommodation services, some personal services, public transport, and masks and protective clothing; VAT reduction from 3% to 1% on the cash accounting scheme for SMEs.
- **Republic of Korea.** Up to a 9-month extension for SMEs filing a tax return and reduced VAT for small businesses with annual turnover below W48 million ($41.35 million).
- **Indonesia.** Income tax exemption for manufacturing workers making less than Rp200 million ($14,300) per year. A waiver on 10% consumption tax on hotels and restaurants in 10 tourist destinations for 3 months.
- **Thailand.** 300% deduction on salary payments made.
- **Japan.** Considering a temporary consumption tax rate reduction from 10% to 5%.

Credit

- **Malaysia.** The Central Bank provided RM2 billion ($486 million) for SMEs loans through commercial banks, supported by a credit guarantee covering 80% of the loan value; also capped the interest rate on special loans at 3.75%.
- **Viet Nam.** Banks to provide an additional D285 trillion ($11 billion) at preferential rates: 0.5–1 percentage point lower than current rates.
- **Cambodia.** $50 million in low-interest loans to SMEs in agriculture through the Rural Development Bank.
- **Japan.** ¥500 billion ($4.57 billion) in lending to micro, small, and medium-sized enterprises (MSMEs) in its first stimulus package (increased to ¥1.6 trillion or about $15 billion in the second package).
- **Philippines.** Loans of up to ₱200,000 ($4,100) for micro businesses and ₱500,000 ($10,400) for SMEs after the lockdown.

Wage Subsidy

Some developed countries (e.g., Australia, Canada, Singapore, Scandinavian countries, and the United Kingdom) provide businesses with 75%–80% of wages of workers who would otherwise be laid off.

Enterprise Pivot

- **Malaysia.** Pivot to import substitution after trade restrictions disrupted the supply chain. The government is now promoting e-commerce to entice people to buy local products, enabling SMEs to earn and slowly embrace digital platforms. It is also increasing internet connectivity in rural areas and encouraging SMEs to tap the global market.

Recommendations

Whatever instruments they deploy, policy makers must ensure that vulnerable SMEs are not left out of the support net. When mapping out a bounce-back strategy, they must take into consideration the immediate implications of COVID-19 on small businesses as the outbreak unfolds, as well as the challenges that will remain once the pandemic is contained and recovery begins.

Here are some recommendations from policy makers:

Pandemic-induced trade restrictions are temporary and must not dissuade small and medium-sized enterprises from tapping the global supply chain. The Sabah state government has been actively promoting exports of Malaysian products even during the lockdown. Trade officials visited Singapore to sell seafood directly before the lockdown. These trade ties encouraged Sabah's aquaculture farmers to experiment with breeding and deep-sea fishing. As part of its import substitution strategy, the government also weaned farmers toward communal farming, even providing guidance on high-value crops to plant. It also enticed investors to come to Sabah and process local timber locally instead of making the state a mere raw materials supplier.

The crisis should further accelerate countries' digital transformation and e-commerce agenda for global trade to flow. Prior to the pandemic, the Asian Development Bank (ADB) has extended loans to help developing member countries increase financial inclusion. Because of the crisis, ADB has modified its assistance to get more SMEs to use digital payments. In the Philippines, digital finance is increasing competition in the financial sector and leading to wider access to funds. Countries must allow global financial technology firms to operate and spur innovation. Governments can also link up payment vendors with businesses and get more small businesses to connect to online platforms to spur trade and economic activity.

The "new normal" should not lower productivity, but rather increase it. The pandemic may have shrunk demand for some products in the international market. The challenge moving forward is sustaining the demand for products and creating new demand as well as new markets. With digitalization, critical processes such as trade registration, inspections, screening, and payments will be hastened.

The private sector must play a part in the bounce-back strategy. Businesses must assist their government in determining how the new normal could take place. They must propose standard procedures conducive to business operations.

Promote the growth of trade corridors. The new normal must lead to greater intra-regional trade as countries slowly relax their trade and border restrictions. Governments must help promote exports, increase internet connectivity, and boost shipping connectivity. In Sabah, the government sets up a free trade zone to promote exports and helps in marketing, branding, and selling the products online.

Resources

Asia Pacific MSME Trade Coalition. 2020. COVID-19 SME Impact Survey.

Foo Ngee Kee. 2020. Support for SMEs to weather the COVID-19 crisis. Presented at ADB's PACER Dialogues. 8 July.

P. Vandenberg. 2020. Bouncing Back Support to SMEs for COVID-19 Recovery. Presented at ADB's PACER Dialogues. 8 July.

P. Vandenberg and M. Helble. 2020. Three Ways to Support Businesses and Their Workers during a Pandemic. *Asian Development Blog.* 3 April.

CHAPTER 2
Protecting the Poor and Vulnerable

Coming Out Stronger from COVID-19: Policy Options on Migrant Health and Immigration

Patrick Duigan
Regional Migration Health Advisor for Asia and the Pacific
International Organization for Migration

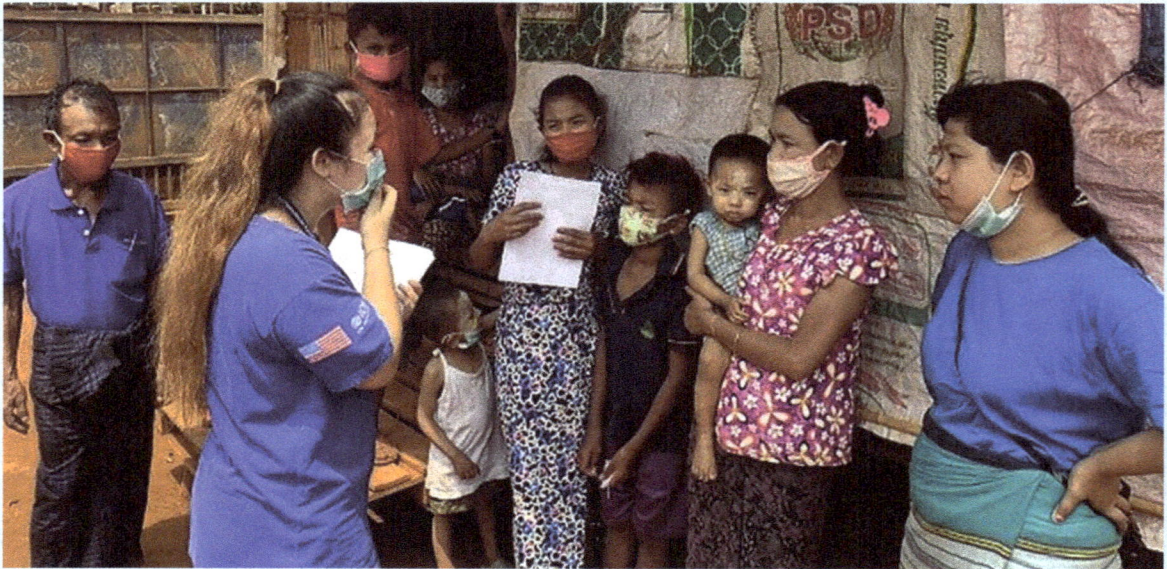

Outreach and health education. The International Organization for Migration (IOM) conducted outreach and health education for migrant families in Mae Sot, Thailand, in April 2020 (photo by IOM).

Introduction

People on the move are among the highly vulnerable groups to the coronavirus disease (COVID-19) crisis. The disproportionate impact on this group, which includes immigrants and those still crossing borders, shows in the unprecedented, multiple challenges they face in health, livelihood, and, for those fleeing war and persecution, access to protection. These challenges heighten their risk of infection, which has implications on the health of their families and communities.

Governments must integrate migrant health and migration policies into their response and recovery efforts. Migrants must have access to COVID-19 health services and be enabled to cope with the pandemic's socioeconomic impacts. Otherwise, their increasing vulnerability could impede efforts to stop the spread of the disease. It is also important to coordinate with governments of host and destination countries on measures targeted at migrants.

Impacts of COVID-19

As of mid-2019, international migrants totaled 272 million, including 164 million workers and 25.9 million refugees (United Nations 2020), but excluding the numerous undocumented migrants. While the extent to which COVID-19 impacts migrants varies, depending on their socioeconomic situation, most count among the most severely hit by the crisis and are at greater risk of infection because of preexisting inequities and vulnerabilities. They are particularly vulnerable to COVID-19 because of the circumstances of their journey and their poor living and working conditions. Impacts bear more heavily on women and children, the elderly, and persons with impairments and/or medical conditions.

Increased health risks. Lockdowns and quarantines have intensified the health risks of refugees and migrant workers living in overcrowded camps, informal settlements, collective shelters, and dormitories, often lacking in water, sanitation, and other basic services. Impacts are greater among irregular migrants, who are forced to move from place to place, stay homeless for prolonged periods, or be confined in cramped detention centers. Rising joblessness, income losses, malnutrition, and food insecurity triggered by the pandemic have also amplified these risks.

Compromised access to health services. Obstacles to migrants' access to health care have heightened with the surge in COVID-19 caseloads and local transmissions. Along with other obstacles, such as migration status, lack of information, absence of health insurance or inadequate finances, and language and cultural barriers, these incidents have deepened their marginalization. Irregular migrants, who are unable or unwilling to access services for fear of detention, deportation, and other punishments, have been particularly impacted. Migrant workers in the informal economy, who often are without contracts and insurances and excluded from social protection schemes, have also been significantly affected.

Rising unemployment and loss of livelihood. The COVID-19-induced economic crisis has cost migrants their jobs and livelihoods. First to go were workers and refugees in the low-wage informal economy. Recent research from the International Labour Organization (ILO) shows that nearly 75% of migrant women and 70% of migrant men were working in the informal sector before COVID-19. The prevalent "last hired, first fired" practice also makes migrant workers in the formal sector more vulnerable to losing their jobs than their native-born counterparts. The unfolding global economic recession, according to ADB, threatens the job security of over 91 million international migrants from Asia and the Pacific.

Declining remittances. Migrants' income losses impact their families and countries of origin. The World Bank estimates that remittances will drop by 20% because of the pandemic, causing hardship to more than 800 million people depending on remittances for much of their subsistence. A sudden stop in remittance flow, according to ADB, could plunge many households in developing Asia—particularly Pacific and Central and West Asian countries—into poverty. The region has at least 10 countries deriving over 10% of their gross domestic product (GDP) from remittances and six of the world's top 10 remittance-recipient countries (ADB 2020).

Implications on Migration

The pandemic has brought new challenges to migration management. Current developments indicate that as countries reopen their borders, they will be imposing additional health requirements for travel, which could result in disproportionate health expenditures and drive more people into irregular migration pathways. Countries could also restrict travel and tourism and limit the potential of migration and human mobility in contributing to development.

Challenges could become much more complex with broader geopolitical and economic contexts coming into play, in addition to changes in the evolutionary patterns of the disease. Against this backdrop, rethinking mobility and migration management, as part of COVID-19 response and recovery measures, assumes critical importance.

Policy Options

A three-track policy agenda may be explored to address the complex challenges posed by COVID-19 to migrant health and immigration. Key considerations that need to inform country policies on each track are outlined below.

1. **Reducing transmission risks**
   A strong case can be made for a migrant-inclusive approach to disease control. Research and empirical evidence show migrants rarely bring infections to their host populations, but denying them care could create risks and lead to higher costs in the long run (British Medical Journal 2019).

   Include migrants in COVID-19 health services. Ensure that all migrants—regardless of their status—have access to the full range of health services to reduce transmission risk. Proactive and innovative measures are needed to break through the current policy and regulatory obstacles that prevent undocumented or irregular migrants from accessing these services.

   Remove obstacles to access to health care. Address stigma and discrimination, language and cultural barriers, and lack of financial resources and information to encourage migrants to seek health care once they feel the symptoms. Provide a range of services to improve their knowledge about the disease, ensure their access to accurate and up-to-date information, build their confidence and communication skills, and strengthen their social support systems. Use social and behavioral change communication to combat xenophobia, racism, and gender and other forms of discrimination. Provide gendered and age and culturally appropriate mental health and psychosocial services and financial assistance, especially to irregular, stranded, laid-off, and other distressed migrants.

   Reduce transmission risks throughout the mobility continuum. Detection of COVID-19 threats has largely improved at border facilities, but more work needs to be done for the spaces of vulnerability where migrants interact with stationary, local communities in their countries of origin, transit, and destination. Engage with community networks, migrant support groups, and migrants themselves to improve prevention education, monitor outbreaks, and facilitate emergency care and treatment in these spaces.

Harmonize and coordinate COVID-19 response across sectors at various governance levels and with governments of host and destination and/or return countries.

2. **Mitigating impacts**

   Address the socioeconomic impacts that erode the ability of migrants and their families to spend for their food and other basic needs, including health care.

   Include all migrants in social protection schemes. Host country governments need to ensure that migrants have access to social protection, including employment-related benefits and social assistance. Provide targeted social assistance tailored to the needs and circumstances of irregular, stranded, and other distressed migrants.

   Mitigate rising job and income insecurity. Host country governments can consider proactively facilitating employment retention of the migrant workforce while creating new jobs for migrant workers in health and other essential services during the pandemic. Economic reintegration activities for returning migrants should be more vigorously undertaken, targeting both employment and entrepreneurship promotion. Ensure the undisrupted flow of remittances.

3. **Leveraging opportunities for transformational changes**

   The opportunity for accelerating progress toward universal health coverage (UHC) has never been as bright, so are the prospects for integrating health into border and mobility management which, like UHC, is crucial to achieving the Sustainable Development Goals. Initial considerations for maximizing these opportunities are discussed below.

   Accelerate universal health coverage progress. Countries could build on their COVID-19 experiences to heighten support for UHC from both the public and private stakeholders, identify the critical gaps in public health systems that need to be improved, determine and implement feasible financing and risk pooling mechanisms, and facilitate the adoption or strengthen implementation of the necessary laws and regulations. Mobilize and train qualified volunteers from the community networks and migrant organizations and support groups that participate in COVID-19 activities in spaces of vulnerability to become the first point of contact for UHC in these areas. Explore incorporating UHC contributions into the payment terms for economic stimulus packages.

   Plan and build capacity for better-managed human mobility and migration. COVID-19 disease modeling suggests that the outbreak's evolution will be context-specific, with infections and mortality burdens taking place on different scales and timelines and in potential multiple waves and clusters (International Organization for Migration [IOM] 2020). This will result in significant variability in the implementation, removal, and possible reintroduction of travel restrictions and border closures worldwide. Therefore, as governments continue to establish health-based border procedures, they need to consider a continually fluctuating situation as well as the measures and capacities in partner countries to manage additional risk. If decisions on cross-border mobility are made without a coordinated, evidence-based assessment of the outbreak across countries, there will be an increased risk of transmission.

Even with full coordination between states, a return to the pre-pandemic mobility levels is unlikely in the short to medium term. Although a full return may also be unlikely in the long term, countries can better manage by adopting a fundamental change in mobility and migration management, taking full account of global health security concerns. Among other things, this means (i) incorporating public health emergency preparedness and response measures into migration management, (ii) adopting a multisector approach, and (iii) strengthening health system capacities for which significant investments need to be made. Within a comprehensive approach to border management that co-opts health imperatives, the IOM's long-standing advocacy for integrating the security and trade perspectives into border management may also be considered.

Policy Implementation

The proposed policy measures require bold political decisions, leadership from the top, strong multisector coordination, and the involvement of migrants as key stakeholders. These requirements may be met through the following institutional arrangements and processes.

Strong political leadership and multisector coordination

An executive or steering committee, comprising senior government officials from immigration, foreign affairs, labor, health, and social welfare departments, and representatives from migrant organizations or their support groups, may be formed as the central decision-making body. A core unit, composed of senior staff from relevant agencies and departments and migrant leaders and advocates, may be established to supervise and coordinate implementation.

Involvement of migrants as key stakeholders

Migrants can participate in decision-making as members of the steering committee and in policy implementation. Migrant participation will be inclusive of all their key networks and organizations.

Partnership and collaboration

The core implementation unit should ensure that other stakeholders will be involved through partnership arrangements, which may be formed based on the spaces of vulnerability and communities where actual work needs to take place. Diaspora organizations and immigrant health professionals will be tapped to support community education and prevention activities as well as provide essential referral services, as needed.

Regional cooperation and development partner support

Build upon existing bilateral and multilateral cooperation among countries to implement the policies and respond to migrant issues and concerns during the COVID-19 crisis and beyond. Multicountry knowledge sharing can support national-level policy implementation and regional cooperation and enhance both as the situation unfolds. Mobilizing and innovating to meet financing needs will be encouraged as a shared responsibility among key stakeholders.

Good Practice Examples

These initiatives provide examples of a migrant-inclusive approach to COVID-19 response and recovery.

Including all migrants in COVID-19 health services

- Portugal has temporarily regularized irregular migrants to ensure their full access to COVID-19 services.
- Peru has approved temporary health coverage for migrants and refugees suspected of or testing positive for COVID-19.
- The United Kingdom has announced that no charges will apply for the diagnosis or treatment of COVID-19 for all foreign visitors, regardless of their residency and immigration status.
- In Lebanon, humanitarian agencies and health partners undertook outreach campaigns to provide information on COVID-19 to refugee populations.
- Singapore has set up medical facilities and triage clinics in migrant workers' dormitories and provided them with food and other necessities, including Wi-Fi.
- City mayors from all over the world, through the Leadership Board of the Mayors Migration Council, are calling on national and international decision makers to commit to an equitable pandemic response and recovery.

Implementing COVID-19 migrant social protection schemes

- The Philippines is providing stipends to migrant workers to ensure that they can still travel when they have valid employment contracts.
- Chile has established the COVID-19 Emergency Stipend for vulnerable migrant families in regular status.
- Malaysia has reduced the migrant worker levy by 25% for employers of workers whose permits expire between April and December 2020.
- New Zealand has made its Wage Subsidy Scheme available to migrants.
- South Africa is providing 30% of its financial support for small convenience shops to foreign-owned businesses, including those owned by refugees.
- Bahrain has established specific responsibilities for private sector employers to ensure appropriate accommodations and facilities for migrant workers during the pandemic.
- In California, a fund is being established to provide income support to migrant workers irrespective of their status.

- The Tunisian Ministry of Social Affairs has issued recommendations to employers, government institutions, and landlords for fair and humane treatment of sub-Saharan migrants and confirmed the provision of in-kind and financial grants to vulnerable migrants and waivers for expiry of work and immigration permits.
- In Bangladesh and Malaysia, the consultancy firm ELEVATE has partnered with several big-name companies in running a helpline to receive and address workers' concerns during the pandemic.

Expanding migrant employment opportunities

- Argentina, Chile, and Peru began allowing foreign-trained refugee doctors, nurses, and others with medical training to work during the COVID-19 response.
- In Ireland, the Medical Council has announced it would allow refugees and asylum-seekers with medical training to help in providing essential medical support by taking up roles, including as health-care assistants.
- In Turkey, the government has long been providing training, certification, and authorization for refugee health professionals to practice in refugee health centers and deliver primary health-care services to refugees free of charge.

Achieving universal health coverage

Thailand has achieved UHC in 2002, the first country to do so, at relatively low cost. The program, which covers 99% of Thai nationals and includes registered migrant workers in the formal sector, has dramatically reduced impoverishment from out-of-pocket payments. It accounts for much of the country's success in flattening the COVID-19 infection curve in late April. Since 2014, UHC has become part of Thailand's comprehensive registration measure to legalize undocumented migrants through nationality verification (Thammatcharee 2020).

Conclusion

By combining mitigation of transmission risks with actions to make migrants less vulnerable to disease, governments will be able to not only protect migrants' health, but also strengthen public health protection. The results of these actions will be far-reaching and beneficial for all: they would speed recovery from COVID-19 and make societies and economies more resilient to pandemics, facilitating overall the attainment of the Sustainable Development Goals.

Resources

H. Canon/ELEVATE. 2020. Migration and Health: Implications of COVID-19 and Private Sector Lessons from Malaysia, Bangladesh, and China, People's Republic of. Presented at ADB's PACER Dialogues. 15 July.

E. Garcetti, Y. Aki-Sawyerr, and B. Covas. 2020. Migrants and Refugees Are Being Forgotten in the COVID-19 Response. This Has to Change. *World Economic Forum*. 12 August.

International Organization for Migration (IOM). 2020. COVID-19 Response Issue Brief: Migration-Related Socioeconomic Impacts of COVID-19 on Developing Countries. *Issue Brief*. No. 1. 12 May.

IOM et al. 2020. The Rights and Health of Refugees, Migrants and Stateless Must Be Protected in COVID-19 Response. Press release. 31 March.

I. Kickbusch and G. Gitahi. 2020. COVID-19 (Coronavirus): Universal Health Coverage in Times of Crisis. *World Bank Blogs*. 29 April.

A. Kikkawa Takenaka et al. 2020. COVID-19 Impact on International Migration, Remittances, and Recipient Households in Developing Asia. *ADB Briefs*. No. 148. Manila: Asian Development Bank.

Lancet Migration. 2020. Leaving No One Behind in the COVID-19 Pandemic: A Call for Urgent Global Action to Include Migrants and Refugees in the COVID-19 Response. Statements: COVID-19 Response. 10 April.

Lancet Migration. Migration and COVID-19 Resources.

H. Legido-Quigley et al. 2019. Healthcare Is Not Universal If Undocumented Migrants Are Excluded. *The BMJ*. 16 September.

A. McDonnell, A.F. Urrutia, and E. Samman. 2019. Reaching Universal Health Coverage: A Political Economy Review of Trends across 49 Countries. *ODI Working Paper*. No. 570. London: Overseas Development Institute.

E. Samman. 2020. *Towards Universal Health Systems in the COVID-19 Era: Opportunities and Threats*. London: Overseas Development Institute.

J. Thammatcharee/National Health Security Office of Thailand. 2020. Thai UHC and COVID-19: New Normal; Leaving No One Behind. Presented at ADB's PACER Dialogues. 15 July.

United Nations. 2020. *Policy Brief: COVID-19 and People on the Move*. New York.

UN Network on Migration. 2020. *Policy Brief: Enhancing Access to Services for Migrants in the Context of COVID-19 Preparedness, Prevention, and Response and Beyond*. Geneva.

World Health Organization (WHO). 2020. Preparedness, Prevention and Control of Coronavirus Disease (COVID-19) for Refugees and Migrants in Non-Camp Settings. Geneva. 17 April.

WHO. Q&A Detail: Universal Health Coverage.

Social Protection Interventions as Medium- and Long-Term Responses to the Pandemic

Valentina Barca and Edward Archibald
Independent Social Protection Experts

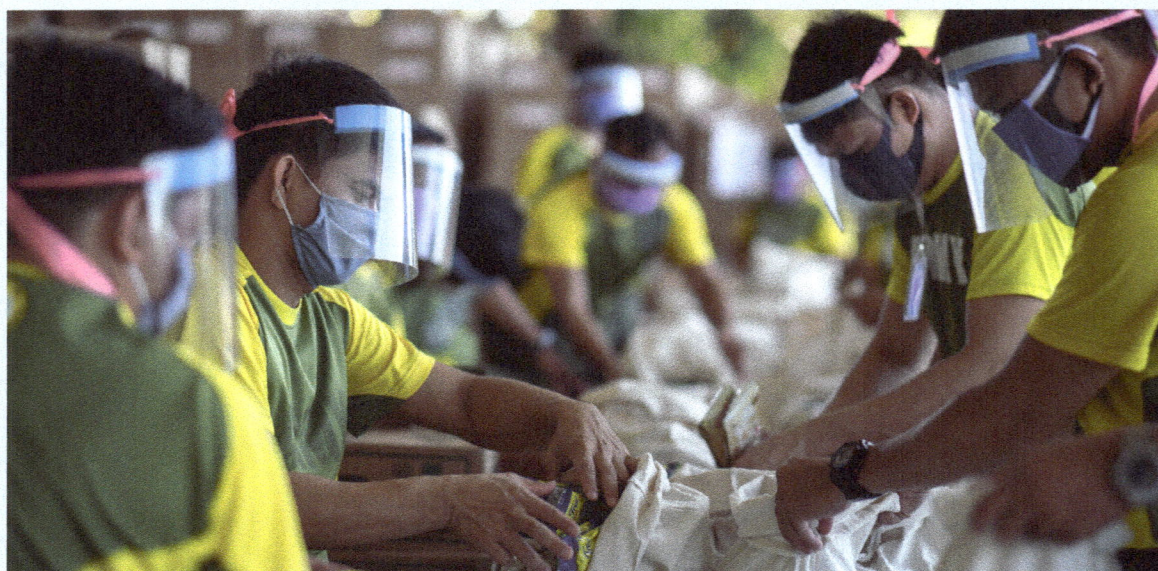

Relief goods distribution. The majority of social protection measures in Southeast Asia are in social assistance, such as cash transfers and relief goods distribution.

Introduction

The coronavirus disease (COVID-19) pandemic presented governments worldwide with a unique set of challenges. The pandemic is a covariate shock unlike anything experienced in recent decades. The impact was extremely swift. There were rapid declines in both supply and demand, affecting extremely high percentages of countries' populations. Mechanisms to reduce physical contact and contagion disrupted service delivery systems. The dimensions of impact include health (e.g., increased mortality and morbidity); economic (e.g., livelihood loss or reduced earnings, supply shortages); and social (e.g., negative coping mechanisms, disruptions to education and health services).

As of July 2020, 200 countries and territories have planned or put in place over a thousand social protection measures in response to COVID-19.[2] These measures include the following categories: social assistance

---

[2] U. Gentilini et al. 2020. *Social Protection and Jobs Responses to COVID-19: A Real-Time Review of Country Measures.* Washington, DC: World Bank.

(noncontributory measures such as cash transfers); social insurance (e.g., unemployment benefits, paid sick leave); and labor market programs (including wage subsidies).

Most countries in Southeast Asia and the People's Republic of China have introduced social protection measures across these three categories. The majority are social assistance measures, particularly the distribution of cash or in-kind transfers.[3]

Members of the Association of Southeast Asian Nations (ASEAN) are also taking a regional approach in protecting vulnerable groups and enhancing household resilience. Recent international commitments include the Declaration of the Special ASEAN Summit on COVID-19[4] and the Joint Statement of the Special ASEAN Ministerial Meeting on Social Welfare and Development on Mitigating Impacts of COVID-19 on Vulnerable Groups in ASEAN.[5]

In East Asia and the Pacific region, social assistance is estimated to represent around 57%, on par with global averages.

In comparison, social insurance responses are more prominent in North America, Europe, and Central Asia, reflecting greater investments in the formalization of social protection over many years.

A United Nations report provides more recent details on social protection responses in Asia and the Pacific.

Policy Design

Policy measures to ensure the resilience and adaptiveness of social protection systems are important in a crisis

It is critical for governments to first ensure the resilience of their social protection systems or programs. This means maintaining routine and effective social protection delivery during the pandemic and preventing the collapse of existing measures in the face of the shock.

Ensuring the resilience of social protection is an active policy choice; it does not necessarily mean maintaining the status quo. The capacity requirements of enforcing conditions are high. Numerous countries have shifted to unconditional transfers combined with intensified messaging and behavioral change communication (which have also shown to be very effective in achieving desired outcomes when accompanying unconditional cash transfers).

---

[3]   Social assistance is generally defined to include a broad range of noncontributory instruments such as poverty-targeted cash transfers; old age and disability social pensions or grants; family and child allowances; public works/workfare; in-kind transfers, stamps, and vouchers; and school feeding.

[4]   ASEAN. 2020. *Declaration of the Special ASEAN Summit on Coronavirus Disease 2019 (COVID-19)*. 14 April.

[5]   ASEAN. 2020. *Joint Statement of the ASEAN Ministerial Meeting on Social Welfare and Development on Mitigating Impacts of COVID-19 on Vulnerable Groups in ASEAN*. 11 June.

It is also fundamental to adapt social protection to cover the changes in context and needs of COVID-19. Adaptation can be through existing or new programs and can be conceptualized as addressing one or more of the following three dimensions (Figure 2.1):

- **Adequacy—the extent to which financial protection adequately addresses risks faced by vulnerable populations (vertical expansions).** Policy options to address COVID-19 needs include (i) providing a higher level of transfer than existing routine social assistance programs, (ii) bringing forward future payments, and (iii) waiving waiting periods.

- **Coverage—the extent to which social protection measures cover the affected population (horizontal expansions).** COVID-19 affects a high percentage of the population. A large proportion of them may live in different geographic areas and have different characteristics (e.g., informal workers) from the "usual" social protection beneficiaries. (The section below elaborates on various options to rapidly expand social assistance caseloads in response to COVID-19.)

- **Comprehensiveness—the extent to which all risks are addressed.** Given the types of needs arising from COVID-19, policy makers can support multidimensional needs by layering or linking additional measures (e.g., to meet health needs, behavioral change objectives, psychosocial support, or protection needs).

Policy Implementation

Figure 2.1: Framing the Policy Dimensions of Shock-Responsive Social Protection

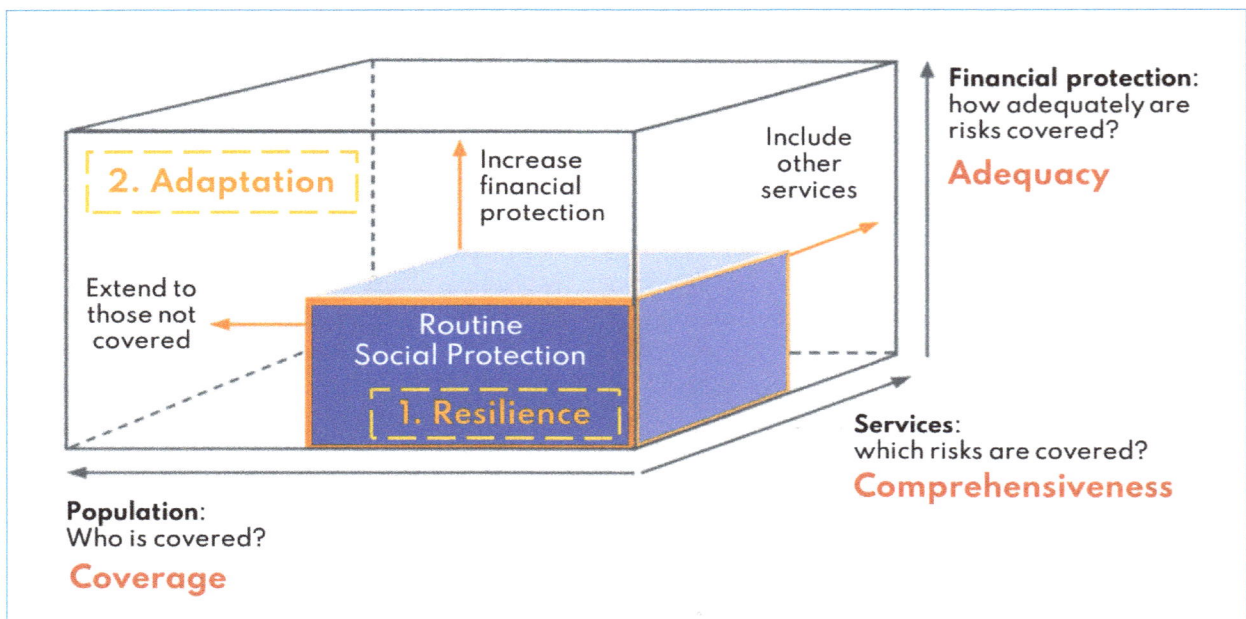

Source: A. Peres. 2020. How Can Social Protection Systems Respond to the COVID-19 Crisis? *Socialprotection.org.* 15 April (adapted from several sources).

Implementing policy decisions to rapidly scale-up social assistance in response to COVID-19

One of the most challenging policy decisions to implement is expanding social assistance in response to COVID-19 via new or existing programs. A central question facing the governments is how those caseloads can most effectively be targeted, registered, enrolled, and paid.

For adding new caseloads, most countries already have something that can be built on for swift coverage, such as

- an existing database (e.g., social registry) that may contain data on potential and past beneficiaries;
- an existing information system linked to that database, potentially with some interoperability or data sharing with other government databases;
- an online form or system for data collection; and
- existing capacity at the local level and tried-and-tested methods for registration.

Having assessed what existing sources or systems can be leveraged, there are several key options to rapidly register and enroll new caseloads:

- using existing data from the social protection sector in creative ways for emergency expansion and payments via a new or existing program;
- using existing data sources beyond the social protection sector in creative ways for emergency registration (e.g., civil registration and vital statistics, national identification data);
- on-demand emergency registration via digital windows and helplines;
- on-demand emergency registration via permanent local offices or capacity; and
- ongoing or periodic active outreach.

Identifying which of these options can be leveraged, and starting with the "easier" approaches, will help ensure timeliness for certain caseloads. Many options are complementary. Implementation can then move to more complex solutions to cover the gaps, potentially in coordination with humanitarian and other non-state actors. Informal workers are particularly challenging to register, but there are opportunities for reaching out to this group.

Whichever option or combination of options is implemented, it is important to ensure adherence to the following dimensions:

- Use **simplified** forms, eligibility criteria, and documentation requirements, and simplified authentication and identification processes, ideally leveraging national identification and civil registration and vital statistics systems, where possible.
- Introduce COVID-19 **contagion control** measures, which may be carried out with the guidance of organizations such as Cash Learning Partnership and HelpAge International.

- Ensure **accessibility for vulnerable groups**, particularly for registrations using on-demand approaches or those which draw on nongovernment sources (e.g., mobile money).

- Responsible use of data at all stages of the chain is required to address the risks of COVID-19, with data being used to roll out technological surveillance and control. A range of approaches ensure respect for data protection and privacy, among others.

There are various mechanisms to transfer payments to new beneficiaries. Two of the most common options are bank accounts and mobile money. Some beneficiaries do not have accounts, but some innovative approaches address this issue.

Outcomes

The extent to which social protection systems were prepared for the scope and scale of COVID-19 is highly variable

While the sheer number of social protection responses by governments appears impressive, these macro-level figures mask an array of challenges on the ground in many countries. The Special Protection Approaches to COVID-19: Expert Advice Helpline has been analyzing COVID-19 response options using some technical tools, including Strategy Decision Matrix and Delivery Systems Matrix. There is significant heterogeneity in the extent of achievement by governments against various dimensions, including the following:

- **Coverage.** The coverage of affected populations has been varied. Access to existing programs has been adapted through relaxed eligibility requirements or on-demand enrollment. New programs cover populations previously not supported. Yet, the global average for increased social protection coverage is just 14%. In East Asia and the Pacific, coverage increased to 60% from 16%, although this figure is driven by a few countries. It is also important to analyze who is covered and who is not.

- **Adequacy.** Many government responses have been constrained by the available budget and an insufficient or nonexistent contingency fund. Transfer sizes are often based on the amount of funding available rather than an assessment of needs. The duration of measures is also important to consider, with most cash transfer interventions being no more than 3 months.

- **Comprehensiveness.** Comprehensiveness has often been lacking in COVID-19 responses, without a strong focus on important needs such as differentiating responses according to individual or household characteristics, and medium-term priorities such as supporting livelihoods and laying the foundations for recovery.

- **Timeliness.** The timeliness of responses has ranged from rapid to very slow. While some countries made payments within a couple of weeks of announcing a measure, others have yet to start payments. Some overly ambitious plans have not thoroughly reflected on the capacities of government and development partners, or the necessary steps for fundamental processes such as targeting and registration.

- **Coordination.** Strong and preexisting coordination mechanisms (including between social protection and humanitarian action) have been leveraged to create a more holistic approach to addressing needs across sectors. Countries that have previously experienced substantial shocks (pre-COVID-19) have often invested in such mechanisms and then leveraged them in response to COVID-19. Many countries, however, have had limited success in coordinating effectively.

- **Gender and social inclusion.** Efforts to address gender and social inclusion appear to have worked well where existing programs have been incorporated into COVID-19 responses, as in Nepal. Women are disproportionally affected by the pandemic, but there has been little evidence to date of programming that targets them.

- **Accountability.** Accountability to affected populations has been limited across many countries and regions, with less emphasis on monitoring, evaluation, and grievance redress mechanisms, which are important for preventing exclusion and inclusion errors, including duplication and/or ghost beneficiaries. Many social protection systems are ill-prepared to address these issues on a rapid and wide scale, but there is often a wealth of local skills and capacity (e.g., in civil society) that can support such functions.

- **Delivery.** A range of delivery systems have been used successfully by some countries to respond to COVID-19, including efforts to leverage the capacity, resources, and systems that exist beyond a social protection program. Some innovative approaches to **registration** have been working well, including online registration in Namibia, South Africa, and Thailand, and the use of data in existing databases on unenrolled households. There have been many advances in **payments**, such as digital government-to-person (G2P) payments in several countries. That said, there have also been a raft of constraints, including lack of interoperability across registries and databases, data protection concerns, and the politicization of registration and targeting.

The degree of preparedness for shocks is a crucial ingredient for success. Where performance against these dimensions has been poor, it is usually in circumstances where social protection systems were not prepared to respond to such a shock.

Recommendations

Looking ahead: recovery from the crisis is likely to be prolonged and incremental

The global economic slowdown and a series of knock-on effects from COVID-19 will compound ongoing mega trends and undermine long-term development goals. There are and will be income losses for households, disrupted supply chains, depreciated exchange rates, and fiscal constraints for many governments because of substantial declines in tax revenues. Many countries will likely see fiscal contraction, tightening financial sector, and reduced bilateral aid.

Food insecurity from loss of income and restrictions to markets and movements will increase, and there may be an increased prospect of fragility, conflict, and violence associated with poorer economic conditions, compromising access to services and income.

In addition, countries and regions will continue to experience increasing intensity and frequency of natural shocks, together with ongoing mega trends such as climate change and migration.

Such scenarios suggest that many households may suffer long-term vulnerability, posing a threat to international and national development goals.

Bold actions in the present will lay strong foundations for the medium and long term

The crisis is an opportunity to advance policy debates on social protection, in turn, creating fiscal space.

Social assistance positively impacts productivity and incomes, alongside social benefits in health, education, and nutrition. Broadening the proportion of citizens who benefit from social protection can also increase the acceptability (strengthened social contract), accountability, and governments' willingness to increase their spending levels accordingly.

There is also a wealth of international evidence on the impact of national social protection responses to COVID-19 and the cost-effectiveness of early action. Governments should take this opportunity to learn and recalibrate existing social protection systems and adapt to the COVID-19 new normal.

Policy and fiscal space should aim to establish more coherent and agile social protection systems. The pandemic has exposed gaps in social protection systems: their inability to cater to expanding needs beyond the "currently poor." There is now a clear rationale for governments to address those weaknesses and build a more comprehensive and joined-up approach across social assistance, social insurance, and labor markets, supported by robust delivery mechanisms.

Many aspects of the informal sector should be formalized as rapidly as possible, adopting suggestions by the International Labour Organization (ILO) (policy responses and social security) and Women in Informal Employment: Globalizing and Organizing. However, such reforms do take time and social assistance will still likely be required to address short-term needs. Localized lockdowns may be especially difficult for certain industries such as tourism and garments. Formalization and enhanced social insurance can mitigate risks for informal or unprotected workers.

In social assistance, the base of potential beneficiaries should be expanded, allowing the social protection system to expand in the event of a crisis, and then contract with lesser affected beneficiaries after the crisis. Focus on those facing the highest barriers and address gender disparities in wages and benefits, access to economic opportunities, and unpaid care work.

Investing in preparedness is nonnegotiable and should be prioritized with appropriate resources. There will be more shocks in the future, whether economic, health, natural, or otherwise, and those countries with prepared systems will be able to support their citizens more efficiently and effectively throughout the distinct—but frequently overlapping—phases of shock cycles (Figure 2.2).[6] Particular attention should be paid to investing in delivery systems such as information systems and mechanisms for targeting, enrollment, registration, payment, and grievance redress, alongside other core elements such as multisector coordination, policies, financing, and

---

[6]   The key stages of a shock are stylized in Figure 2.2, illustrating that the beginning of a new stage does not necessarily mean the end of the previous. Clearly, this stylization will differ according to the type of shock (e.g., a protracted crisis). Figure 2.2 also illustrates how different shocks often overlap within a country and follow distinct patterns (e.g., recurrences) over time—meaning any strategy to address these needs to look across different shocks and their cycles in the short, medium, and long term.

the involvement of local actors. TRANSFORM provides step-by-step guidance and learning materials on shock-responsive social protection (see Chapter 3 especially).

Figure 2.2: A Stylized Illustration of the Patterns of Shock Cycles

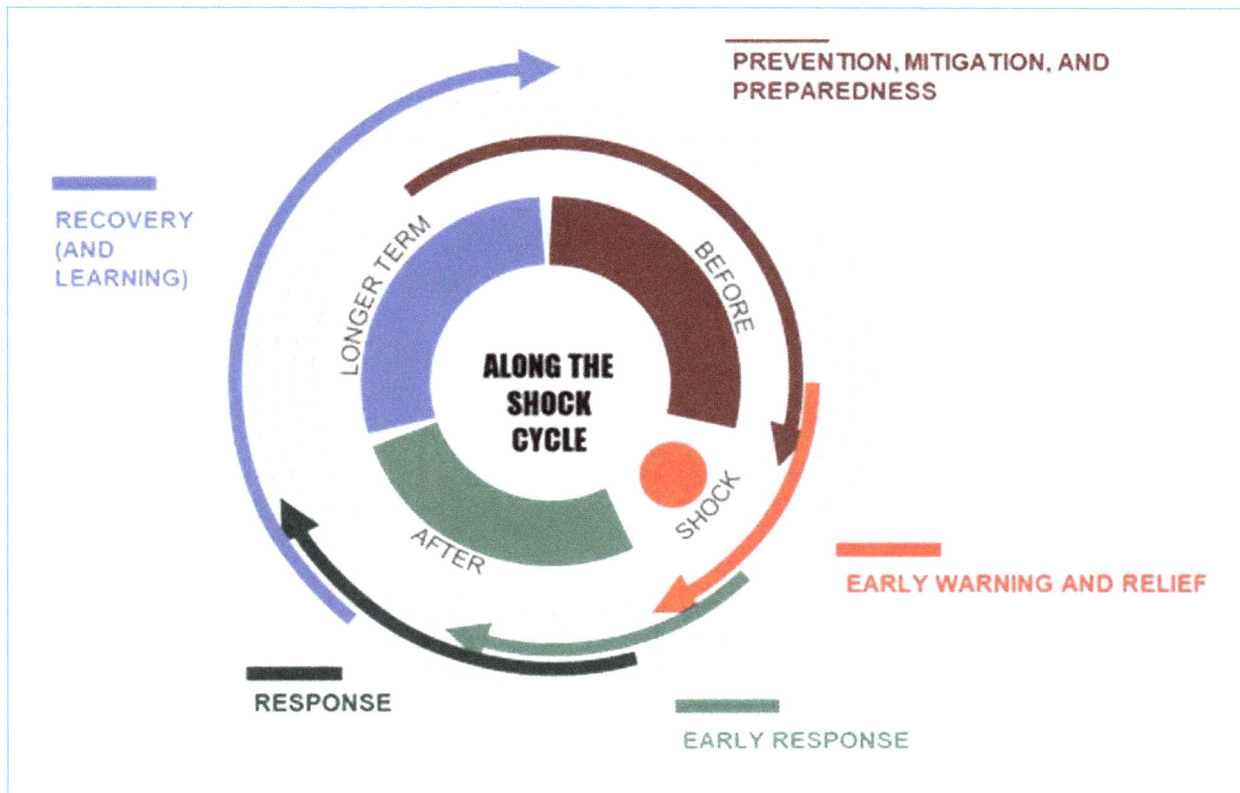

PREVENTION, MITIGATION, AND PREPAREDNESS

RECOVERY (AND LEARNING)

LONGER TERM

BEFORE

ALONG THE SHOCK CYCLE

SHOCK

AFTER

EARLY WARNING AND RELIEF

RESPONSE

EARLY RESPONSE

Source: R. Beazley et al. 2019. *Study on Shock-Responsive Social Protection in Latin America and the Caribbean: Summary of Key Findings and Policy Recommendations*. Oxford: Oxford Policy Management and World Food Programme.

Overall, while the challenges may loom large, the current crisis presents an opportunity to make sound investments that will reap strong dividends in the future. Social protection should be viewed as an integral component of a long-term, sustainable development strategy. Public expenditure on social protection averages 20% of GDP in Organisation for Economic Co-operation and Development countries. The decisions recommended above will require trade-offs, and governments should be realistic in their plans and adapt their approaches to specific contexts. Despite the enormity and gravity of the COVID-19 pandemic, it presents a small opening for bold decision-making that can lay a foundation for future generations to prosper, thrive, and weather the storm.

Resources

ASEAN. 2020. *Declaration of the Special ASEAN Summit on Coronavirus Disease 2019 (COVID-19)*. 14 April.

_____. 2020. *Joint Statement of the Special ASEAN Ministerial Meeting on Social Welfare and Development on Mitigating Impacts of COVID-19 on Vulnerable Groups in ASEAN*. 11 June.

V. Barca et al. 2020. *A Conceptual Framework Based on Shock Responsive Social Protection Systems*. Presentation given via socialprotection.org. 7 April.

V. Barca and M. Hebbar. 2020. *On-Demand and Up-to-Date? Dynamic Inclusion and Data Updating for Social Assistance.* Bonn: Deutsche Gesellschaft für Internationale Zusammenarbeit (GIZ).

R. Beazley et al. 2019. *Study on Shock-Responsive Social Protection in Latin America and the Caribbean: Summary of Key Findings and Policy Recommendations*. Oxford: Oxford Policy Management and World Food Programme.

U. Gentilini et al. 2020. *Social Protection and Jobs Responses to COVID-19: A Real-Time Review of Country Measures*. Washington, DC: World Bank.

Organisation for Economic Co-operation and Development. 2020. Social Spending (indicator) (accessed 23 August 2020).

United Nations. 2020a. *Policy Brief: The Impact of COVID-19 on South-East Asia*. July 2020.

_____. 2020b. *Social Protection Responses to COVID-19 in Asia and the Pacific: The Story So Far and Future Considerations*. Bangkok.

CHAPTER 3
Accelerating Digital Transformation

Building the Infrastructure for Digital Finance during COVID-19 and Beyond

David Lee Kuo Chuen*

Professor
Singapore University of Social Sciences

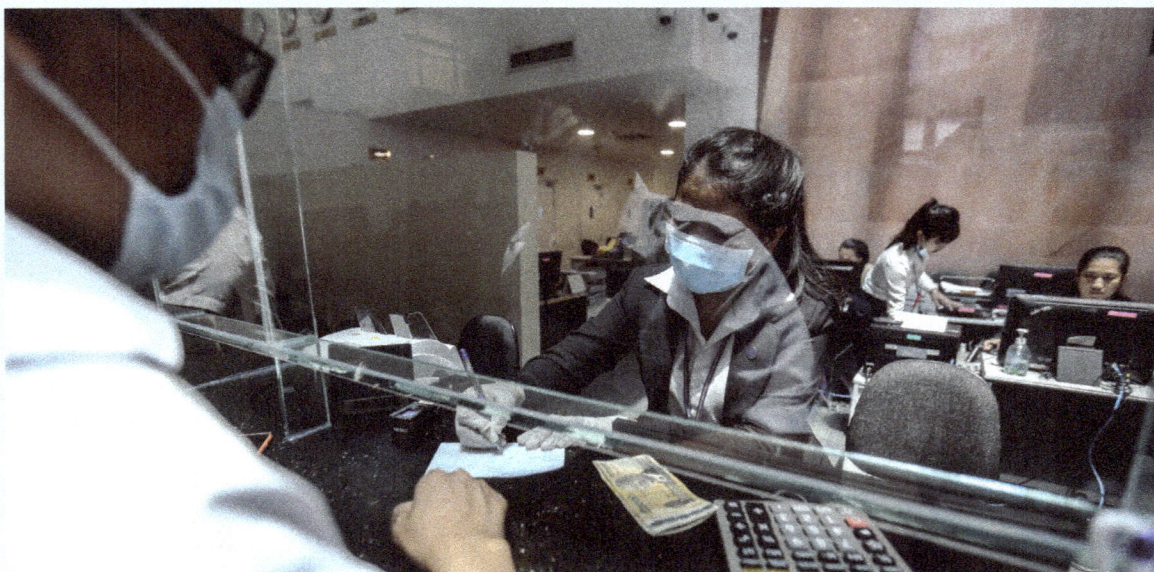

Interrupted cash flow. The COVID-19 pandemic has disrupted cash flows, including payments, investments, and remittances.

Introduction

The coronavirus disease (COVID-19) pandemic has changed the world significantly. The Asian Development Bank (ADB) estimates the global economic impact of the crisis to be between $5.8 trillion and $9.1 trillion. Border closures have disrupted traditional sources of cash flow, jeopardizing such industries as travel and hospitality, beauty, fashion, and retail. External cash flows have declined with the decrease in the number of tourists and business travelers and reduced foreign income from remittances, supply chains, e-commerce, and investments. This decline further leads to lower internal consumption and debt servicing abilities that may result in layoffs and disrupt operation and governance.

COVID-19 is also accelerating global digital transformation and exposing many challenges. Since the outbreak, broadband service providers have seen up to a 60% increase in internet traffic. Services are switching to

---

*   This policy brief was written with the support of ADB's Finance Sector Group (Junkyu Lee, Lisette Cipriano, and Jae Deuk Lee).

online operation and communication in response to mobility and contact restrictions. This situation calls for an immediate allocation of resources to build the national and regional digital infrastructure, which should be classified as a public good expenditure to provide everyone access. A contactless connection is key to addressing telecommunication and inclusive fintech bottlenecks. Mesh networks with satellite and digital identification are feasible solutions to create business opportunities, enable a lower marginal cost of network expansion, and accelerate digital finance infrastructure.

Challenges

First, there is a lack of public infrastructure and regulations that enable contactless connection, which is aggravated by the gap in digital knowledge and infrastructure. Meanwhile, more opportunities lie in emerging markets, and funding for infrastructure, start-ups, and education remains vital.

Second, the fundamental determinant of financial inclusion and e-inclusion is the telecommunication infrastructure. Many countries such as the People's Republic of China and the Republic of Korea have been investing heavily in 5G, the next generation of wireless network technology. It has faster speed and greater bandwidth, enabling more connected devices and reducing latency to virtually zero. Edge computing is also rising along with 5G. It does computing closer to the source of data and allows more personalized services, and it will have lots of advantages when integrated with 5G.

Providing access to the digital infrastructure can improve social welfare, enhance resilience, increase national competitiveness, and facilitate international trade. However, the reality is that over 3 billion people, or 41% of the world population, do not have internet access, and the situation in Asia is even worse. The primary reasons behind this digital divide are cost and scalability, especially in rural areas. These issues should be addressed in pursuing cheaper, more inclusive alternatives.

Technology Solutions

1. **5G versus mesh network**

   A mesh network is a cheaper alternative to 5G and edge computing. It refers to a group of devices or nodes that act as a single Wi-Fi network, and it can provide multiple Wi-Fi sources in a faster, smoother, and more reliable way. A critical advantage of the mesh network is that it can expand with less technical or financial hindrance. This scalable solution is especially beneficial in places with poor connection and remote areas with limited internet infrastructure. It is the most crucial first step in e-inclusion for financial services.

2. **Cellular network versus satellite**

   A cellular repeater amplifies the signal and improves connectivity using a donor antenna that receives and transmits the signal from nearby cell towers. Another option is to connect a node of the mesh network to a satellite, which provides a more affordable connection to the internet for an entire area network in remote areas. It is an alternative source of contactless connection that enhances the traceability of products or changes related to crop growth and farming conditions. Data and information on farmers and crops provide transparency and reduce the risk for micro insurers and lenders, improving branding and quality, which are essential for leveling the supply chain playing field for emerging and agriculture economies.

3. **Digitizing fiat currency**

Digitizing fiat currency can create sustainable and new fintech models. Central bank digital currencies (CBDCs) may propel a cheaper form of remittances and delivery versus payments, and their use means more than improved speed and efficiency in the payment system and exchange of value. From in-country CBDC, the follow-on second stage will be regional cooperation of CBDCs as a critical element of cross-border remittance capabilities. The next stage will be to foster the growth of regional digital infrastructure to facilitate digital trades.

By connecting the unconnected and digitizing fiat currency, there will be more transparency for a more equitable and sustainable economy. Privacy can be maintained, but funding and education are the most challenging issues.

Network Cost and Effects

From the cost and benefit perspective, the initial infrastructure cost will have to be borne by individual countries. Network externalities from the local and regional digital infrastructure may prevent individual domestic material consumptions from burdening the neighboring economies. If these burdens exceed the cost of funding regional digital infrastructure, it calls for government incentives and subsidies for infrastructure building and users' participation, with the appropriate rules and regulations.

The local digital infrastructure builds the local network, which is dependent on the strength and size of the user base. An increase in usage and users leads to a direct network effect, increasing new products and services for other users. The increase in value through the local and direct network incentivizes further growth of the ecosystem.

Collaborative efforts may result in a positive feedback network effect to the region by developing distributed ledger technology and industry standards in communication, trade, tourism, health care, supply chain, payments, and remittances. More regional and global participants may lead to many new entrants, giving a more extensive and diverse choice of products, services, and customers.

These three network effects (local, direct, and feedback) may stimulate investment in anticipation of higher returns. Higher investment may lead to access to cheap capital with more contactless connectivity and cross-border activities. These positive network externalities give rise to a positive loop. In the early stage of the development cycle, international agencies such as ADB may provide funding and financing before the network effects kick in.

Policy Options

Governance

Digital infrastructure spans across different ministries involving telecommunication, monetary, economic and enterprise development, trade, education, and treasury. Some countries have a coordinating minister or a smart nation division under the Prime Minister's office. The longer-term solution is to have a ministry designated as the digital infrastructure and trade ministry.

There are many challenges in implementing a digital policy. It involves the granting of telecommunication licenses for the satellite and the mesh network and payments licenses. Taxation of digital assets and services needs clear guidelines from the treasury. Grants for education and the building up of skills and knowledge are needed. Trade and industry cooperation in the region requires negotiation with other countries. Private sector development needs to be driven by grants and subsidies.

Grants and education

Grants and education play an important role in facilitating the development of fintech and digitalization. COVID-19 provides opportunities for fintech companies and start-ups to scale-up and provide solutions, but education and grants are needed to help businesses transform and collaborate.

The purpose of grants is twofold: to ensure sustenance and growth in fintech and to foster acceleration and upskilling in digitalization. The first will help reduce layoffs in the short term and improve the growth of the priority sectors in the long term. The second can help businesses create products to serve new customers and make digital services user-friendly, which is important for inclusion and scalability. Governments can also offer training allowances for approved and relevant courses. Universities will need to revamp their syllabus and include more digital materials.

Access for all

Digital inclusion provides the most appropriate option. It is low-cost, sustainable, and scalable. Those who lack digital access represent the most significant demand and unexplored markets in this pandemic.

Convert dead assets to live and tradable assets. Regulation should encourage the digitization of non-securities while bearing in mind appropriate risk-mitigating measures. Then digital assets for trading can be fractionalized and heterogenized (differentiated). The economy can leapfrog via these exchanges that deal with delivery versus payments to the region and beyond.

The ultimate goal of serving the underserved will be achieved eventually with linkages to international markets.

Digital infrastructure as a public good

National digital infrastructure is vital in accelerating financial services for inclusion. Nations can focus on building technologies related to the mesh satellite or 3G/4G/5G network, virtual asset service providers' open platforms, CBDC, and open data. In the meantime, a regional digital infrastructure is key to facilitating a cheaper, secure, and sustainable source of remittances; e-trading of digital assets; and access to cheap capital.

There needs to be a focus on network externalities to foster alignment and collaboration domestically and beyond. This may be the only way to lift the economy from the COVID-19 crisis toward sustainable recovery with contactless connectivity. It is recommended that ADB assess the opportunities in filling the gap in investment needs to foster the national and regional digital infrastructure.

Policy Implementation

Nearly all the policies above are in various stages of implementation by different countries. Their execution and effects are summarized below.

5G and edge computing

By 2023, 5G will make up around one-fifth of all mobile data traffic, with 25% of the use cases depending on edge computing capabilities. The integration of 5G and edge computing will also bring several benefits to mobile video viewing.

Mesh network

Several entities across different jurisdictions have experimented on the mesh network, which is the cheaper and more inclusive alternative. The SmartMesh project team is implementing the mesh network in the Philippines. The MeshBox Tesla model has passed all the necessary hurdles to get a license from the Federal Communications Commission last August. The Singapore University of Social Sciences is experimenting on a mesh network and MeshBox on campus, and the program will be expanded to other higher learning institutions in the country.

As the production scales, the unit cost of a MeshBox will drop from the current $1,000. Mesh is still a nascent technology, but there is good potential.

Satellite

Satellites have been used in analyzing financial data from remotely located farmers. Rabobank and Wageningen University, for example, finished a pilot in Ethiopia using the Climate Smart Digital Farm Finance Solution tool to provide banks with data on smallholders' crop production, which reduced the need to visit farms in remote areas. Other projects pioneer in offering lower-cost financial products to previously unreachable farmers. These examples show how satellites can provide affordable and secured solutions for money transfer in remote areas.

Central bank digital currency

The Monetary Authority of Singapore has engaged various stakeholders to issue CBDC using distributed ledger technology. Project Ubin involved the tokenization of the Singapore dollar and cooperation with commercial banks, central banks, and technology companies in settlement. The project highlights not just the ability to realize cross-border remittance and tokenize assets transfer, but also the role of government policies in spearheading tokenization and regional cooperation in the exchange of value.

The Monetary Authority of Singapore, JPMorgan, and Temasek have developed a blockchain payments system that handles different currencies on the same network. Other projects seeded by the Government of Singapore for digital identity include AID:Tech, which works with Women's World Banking to provide microinsurance to underinsured women. Affinity, a portable digital identity technology provider, and GeTs with TradeTrust are working on cross-border trade documentation and agreements on the blockchain. The idea of identity systems as a building block to development is gaining traction, and ADB is at the forefront of this initiative. Self-sovereign identity is an extension of that idea with portability.

The People's Republic of China has already completed the back-end infrastructure of its CBDC, which is called Digital Currency Electronic Payment. The Digital Currency Electronic Payment wallet will support major functions, including digital asset exchange, wallet management, ability to look up past transactions, and offline payment via QR code. There are several initiatives to digitize assets using distributed ledger technology or blockchain.

The use of distributed ledger technology allows Cambodia to leapfrog the traditional means of connecting all players and address real-time gross settlement. Project Bakong links all payment service providers into one system via an open API, enabling users to transact peer-to-peer securely without transaction fees in real time.

Project Inthanon is into the third phase as a collaboration between the Bank of Thailand and eight financial institutions. Project Inthanon-LionRock was a project initiated by the monetary authority of Hong Kong, China and the Bank of Thailand to explore real-time cross-border funds transfers and foreign exchange transactions via a corridor network to achieve payment versus payment more efficiently.

The experience from these countries is that unless there is a need for financial inclusion and to prevent fraud, the financial institutions are unlikely to collaborate as willingly. There is an opportunity for emerging economies to leapfrog as the number of underserved determines the value of a digital infrastructure project.

Recommendations

In line with the policies discussed, the following action plans are recommended in addition to 10 enablers of digital inclusion to be implemented during the pandemic.

Stay connected

In lieu of the increase in telecommunication and network usage, network operators should prepare for the high demand, manage the communication facilities, keep track of the key network infrastructure service performance, and prevent congestion.

Connect the unconnected

One affordable way to ensure connection is through the deployment of satellite and mesh network. Create a favorable regulatory environment, such as a blanket license policy, cost-based license fee, and reduced import duties on satellite equipment to encourage uptake and deployment of satellite services.

This policy brief has not discussed portable identity and decentralized technology in depth despite the initiatives of Temasek Holdings in portable identities (also known as Self-Sovereign Identities) and the Government of the People's Republic of China in the Blockchain-based Service Network (BSN) for small and medium-sized enterprises (SMEs). Such democratized efforts in identities and distributed ledger are crucial. ADB should lead the discussions to ensure interoperability and collaboration for the region.

Ten Enablers of Digital Inclusion

Policy makers should look into these critical enablers for digital inclusion and provide support for businesses to transform, cope with the challenges and pain points, and use the opportunities associated with COVID-19 to enable the economy to leapfrog and serve the underserved.

1. **Fast, stable internet, mobile, and mesh network connectivity**

   Use 3G/4G/5G, satellite, and mesh network for connectivity. Democratized connectivity goes beyond affordability.

2. **Interoperable value transfer gateway**

   Enable low-cost, real-time transfer and settlement through interoperable systems.

3. **Privacy protection for users**

   Combine processes that govern hygienic behavior with the latest technologies, such as secret sharing, secured multiparty computing, zero-knowledge proof, trusted executable environment, and other cryptography and encryption standards.

4. **Strong security framework**

   Put in place a trust distribution process in software and hardware to ensure no single point of failure or attack. There is a strong case for legislation and regulation to require setting up a technology risk management committee in licensed and listed institutions with specific skills and understanding of the risk and complexity of nascent and scalable technology.

5. **Open source and trust distribution governance**

   Regulation and processes for the distribution of trust should be encouraged. There is also a need to promote open source and open environment for apps, data, and systems to crowdsource wisdom, defense, and resources to guide against malicious attacks and maintain an equitable environment for digital assets.

6. **Digital literacy and user experience**

   Education remains a priority. Software and hardware companies can improve user experience to ensure that the learning curve is shortened by functional interfaces and guidance from the devices.

7. **Portable digital identity**

   The identity of individuals and organizations now extends beyond foundational components such as national identity and includes credentials and history relating to employment and finance. However, the data are typically constrained either by lack of digitization or portability across platforms and borders. User-centric solutions such as portable digital identity (or self-sovereign identity) can ensure portability and fair exchange of value. There is also a need to establish new data sharing guidelines.

8. **Easy compliance**

   Revise, update, and enhance existing regulations, rules, and guidelines in line with new developments. It is crucial for the ministries or departments involved to coordinate changes. A sandbox environment may provide temporary relief and limit systematic risk.

9. **Comprehensive data and oracle ecosystem**

   Digital assets are a digital representation of physical or virtual goods and services. Storage and processing capabilities determine the competitiveness of an economy and sector. When a smart contract is used, an external source of data or blockchain to record transactions is crucial for the proper functioning of decentralized apps. Such an oracle ecosystem is needed to provide data, and a national digital infrastructure will be useful for this purpose.

10. **Talent, knowledge, and skills**

    Education systems in urban and rural areas are substantially different. As the digital economy develops, the need for talents, knowledge, and skills at all levels will be enormous.
    The democratization of communication services will enhance the ability of talents to learn via the internet. Rural areas will benefit the most from making knowledge acquisition, on-the-job training, and internships accessible online to anyone anywhere.

Resources

Altencalsoft. 2020. How Edge Computing Is Revolutionising the Telecom Industry.

H. Baharudin. 2020. Parliament: More Jobs in Digital Sector; Businesses to Receive Bonus for Adopting Digital Solutions, Says Iswaran. *The Straits Times*. 4 June.

E. Becker. 2020. How Hard Will the Coronavirus Hit the Travel Industry? *National Geographic*. 3 April.

Boxmining. 2020. China's National Digital Currency DCEP/CBDC Overview.

Deloitte and Monetary Authority of Singapore. 2017. *The Future Is Here. Project Ubin: SGD on Distributed Ledger.* Monetary Authority of Singapore.

C. Duffy. 2020. What Is 5G? Your Questions Answered. *CNN*. 6 March.

EMEA Satellite Operators Association. Enabling Digital Financial Inclusion through Satellite Communication.

Ericsson. Edge Computing—A Must for 5G Success.

Financial Times. 2020. Loss of Working Hours to Equal 195M Full-Time Jobs, UN Agency Warns. 7 April.

G. Fleishman. 2020. Wireless Mesh Networks: Everything You Need to Know. *PCWorld*. 5 May.

N. Gan and D. Culver. 2020. China Is Fighting the Coronavirus with a Digital QR Code. Here's How It Works. *CNN*. 16 April.

N. Glazebrook. 2020. How 5G and Edge Computing Will Change the Telecom Industry in 2020. *The Fast Mode*. 24 February.

Global Times. 2020. China Ramping up Research into 6G.

J. Greevink. 2019. 3 Ways Satellite Tech Is Helping to Transform Finance. *GEO Awesomeness*. 6 June.

J. Hildenbrand. 2016. How Wi-Fi Mesh Networks Work. *Android Central*. 13 October.

Monetary Authority of Singapore. Project Ubin: Central Bank Digital Money Using Distributed Ledger Technology.

National University of Singapore. 2020. *FAQs on COVID-19 Outbreak*.

Organisation for Economic Co-operation and Development. 2020. *Keeping the Internet Up and Running in Times of Crisis*. 4 May.

Qualcomm. Everything You Need to Know about 5G.

C. Setboonsarng. 2020. Tourism-Reliant Thailand Shelves 'Travel Bubble' Plan as Asia Virus Cases Rise. *Reuters*. 6 August.

Statista. Global Digital Users Worldwide as of July 2020.

Wikipedia. Wireless Mesh Network. Last modified 27 January 2021, 04:54 (UTC).

World Bank. 2020. *The Global Economic Outlook During the COVID-19 Pandemic: A Changed World*. 8 June.

Fostering Resilient Start-Up Ecosystems in the New Normal

Arndt Husar
Senior Public Management Specialist (Digital Transformation)
Digital Technology for Development Unit, Asian Development Bank

A fledgling company. Start-ups can serve as building blocks for the digital transformation of industries and economies (photo by iStock/Yue).

Introduction

Start-ups come in many shapes, forms, and stages of maturity. The technology "unicorns" are companies valued at more than $1 billion and backed by massive private equity funds. However, many are entrepreneurs and early-stage start-ups still testing the market for their business idea and prototyping their solutions.

The coronavirus disease (COVID-19) pandemic has triggered a fresh wave of digitalization. However, it has not lifted all boats, and many small start-ups are struggling to remain afloat. Short on capital, they are forced to let talents go, abandon innovation processes that are not yet profitable, and focus on survival. In the meantime, larger and well-funded start-ups are re-strategizing, with some switching to a more restrictive hiring approach or even letting go of staff.

Measures are needed to preserve start-up ecosystems, as they play an important role in the digital transformation of economies. These measures include financial assistance, incentives, and a conducive policy environment for the growth of start-ups. Regional collaboration among ecosystem developers can also help promote knowledge sharing and best practices in crisis response.

Context

Start-ups attract talent and funding, catalyze local innovation, and create jobs. At the same time, they help transform economies by driving innovation and collaborating with traditional sectors to increase productivity and competitiveness of their legacy systems. Research of the Kauffman Foundation shows that nearly all net job creation in the United States (US) comes from new and young companies, especially scalable ones.

A conducive ecosystem—made up of entrepreneurs, talents, enablers, and funders—is crucial for the emergence of viable start-ups and its global connectedness essential for reaching scale.

Asia accounts for 30% of the world's top-ranking ecosystems, which are still concentrated in more developed countries. Governments that realize the value of fostering entrepreneurship have been active enablers through policies and incentives as well as early-stage funders.

In terms of cities, four of the top 20 emerging ecosystems are in Asia: Mumbai (#1), Jakarta (#2), Guangzhou (#6), and Kuala Lumpur (#11) based on the Global Startup Ecosystems Report 2020.

In Southeast Asia, most ecosystems are still in the early development phase ("activation"), but Kuala Lumpur and Jakarta have already entered the next phase ("globalization"), given their size and rapid development.

Singapore is a leader in the region, benefiting from its position as a regional hub for the finance industry and as the regional headquarters of multinationals. The government has actively attracted and collaborated with venture capitalists. Its supportive policies, incentives, and dedicated programs contributed to the success of its start-up ecosystem. Runner-up ecosystems around the region are currently profiting from access to tech talent, entrepreneurs, and market opportunities.

However, between March and June 2020, 39% of Southeast Asian start-ups reported less than 3 months of financial runway, putting their viability at risk. Data on fundraising show that there have been significant disruptions, but agile entrepreneurs have some opportunities to tailor their solutions to the current context. Venture capital investments had dropped off drastically, but have since recovered. The strength and resilience of an ecosystem lie partly in the numbers. Therefore, assistance to start-ups in this time of crisis is crucial to defend hard-won gains, retain the globally mobile talents they employ, and secure a slice of the digital economy cake.

Policy Design

Automation, increased connectivity, and material science are transforming our economy, while the COVID-19 pandemic is pushing us toward a "new normal" even in noneconomic spheres such as entertainment, tourism, and education. As emerging economies embrace and adjust to post-industrial realities and traditional employment relationships become more fragile, the remaining bright spots that the young generation can turn to are digital innovation and entrepreneurship.

The following policy priorities are not very different from measures that experts recommended prior to the pandemic, but have become pressing given the worrying trends described above:

1. **Rush to save start-ups**

   Partner with venture capitalists and angel investors by providing a quick injection of equity capital through matching funds and/or investor tax credits to protect the 6-month financial runway of viable start-ups. Effective ecosystems require a well-calibrated start-up funnel in which all generations—early-, mid-, and late-stage companies—play their role and interact. Funding may need to be designed differently for different market segments and prioritized to encourage the ecosystem's specialization or to protect a particularly affected market segment.

2. **Keep start-up talent**

   Building a pool of experienced talents takes years and a lot of resources. Take action to prevent them from leaving the city, region, or country by helping start-ups retain and attract talents during the pandemic and beyond.

3. **Protect and harness specialization**

   Many ecosystems have evolved specialized clusters with competitive advantages that are promising for future growth. Start-ups that develop technology based on scientific advances and high-tech engineering innovations take longer to evolve their clusters and are hard-won assets.

4. **Spur demand**

   During the crisis, when clients are cutting costs, the government is often among the few remaining buyers. Public procurement can help fill the gap and use the opportunity to accelerate the adoption of innovative solutions. Another option is to spur the demand for innovative products and services by providing financial incentives for modernization in the private sector (e.g., digitalization and automation).

5. **Support the start-up infrastructure**

   Keep alive support programs (e.g., incubators, accelerators, scale-up initiatives, and mentorships) that drive quality for scaling and help transition start-ups into the new normal. An ingredient for success is a regulatory environment that facilitates the growth of new technology clusters. Reform and systemic improvements, such as digital identification and interoperable payment systems, should not pause, but accelerate during a crisis.

Policy Implementation

These policies require a concerted effort among different departments or agencies of the government. The incentive system and regulatory environment in which many start-ups operate cut across various government levels—from the subnational level (e.g., free or low-cost office space in tech parks) to the national level (e.g., entrepreneur and talent visas).

Building a framework for supporting start-ups is largely a subnational agenda, and metropolitan areas are often in healthy competition with each other and with regional and international players. Local governments tend to take a convening and enabling role and work with a wide range of partners such as educational and research and development (R&D) institutions (as producers of talent), investors (as financiers and advisors), the private sector (as potential clients), as well as start-up support organizations and advisors (involved in scouting, mentoring, community building, or branding).

Ecosystem developers should focus on strengthening local resources and the network. As ecosystems evolve, resources become critical in triggering start-up success. In the world of start-up ecosystems, success begets success. Large start-up "exits" (i.e., acquisition by another company) and rising valuations drive the accumulation of start-up know-how and resources, which create a virtuous cycle of ecosystem success. When weighing the costs of a focused intervention during this crisis, governments should consider saving start-up jobs via equity-based funding rather than saving jobs in small businesses through grants. Research by Startup Genome shows the cost savings can be up to 41%.

Countries can use the crisis as an opportunity to transform the economy and bet on future-ready start-ups. This strategy offers a cost-effective way of achieving economic competitiveness in the new normal. This will create high-tech jobs, which have a high employment multiplier effect.

Examples of COVID-19 Response

What are governments doing to support start-up ecosystems during the crisis?

Singapore has organized its response around (i) providing additional funding via an equity top-up program, bridge financing, and working capital loans; (ii) ensuring talent retention through wage subsidies, increased funding for job creation, and a traineeship program; and (iii) supporting activities that create opportunities for investment deals and continued innovation. Other ecosystem actors also sprang into action by collating relevant information online and convening virtual meetups. One result is a list of laid-off start-up employees to connect them with companies that are still hiring. Start-ups, therefore, have considerable support to adjust, pivot, and evolve their business model.

In Malaysia, tech start-ups could access a funding relief facility via Malaysia Debt Ventures, which accept applications for cash flow support from venture capitalists and government-backed tech start-ups to sustain their operations. In addition, the Digital Economy Corporation has launched an investor matching initiative with more than 70 investors. It ran an alternative funding campaign for young start-ups that cannot access special relief funds. It is also rallying tech start-ups and features targeted solutions and knowledge resources to help businesses and the public weather the crisis.

Further afield, the Government of the United Kingdom has placed an equity support fund called the Coronavirus Future Fund. It targets pre-revenue and pre-profit companies in the United Kingdom that rely on equity investment and provides government convertible loans ranging from roughly $150,000 to $6 million. Future Fund loans can be matched with at least an equal amount of funding by private equity investors.

Germany launched a suite of support programs to the tune of €2 billion ($2.5 billion) for start-ups and SMEs, apart from the broad-based labor market response. Its Corona Matching Facility targets venture capital fund-backed start-ups and young growth companies. Eligible private fund managers can apply for financing to match funding rounds. There are additional facilities available via the Corona Liquidity Facility that bundles available investment capital support programs. For early-stage start-ups that have not yet mobilized investment capital, a second pillar with equity and subsidy support is available.

Recommendations

Saving start-ups can help transition the wider economy toward a new normal and put it on the path of digital transformation.

Countries with dedicated agencies for entrepreneurship development and/or start-up support and policy linkages with relevant departments are at an advantage, as they can quickly launch crosscutting actions. Others should consider designating a lead agency with the institutional power to compose and launch a start-up-focused COVID-19 response program without delay.

Cities in the region and within the same stage of the start-up life cycle may find knowledge sharing with their peers valuable. Ecosystem developers may benefit from the insights and expertise of founders and business mentors, particularly from an advanced ecosystem, such as Beijing, Seoul, Singapore, Shanghai, or Tokyo.

Resources

Action Community for Entrepreneurship (ACE). 2020. *Info Package for Startups*. April.

ACE. 2020. Supporting Startups amid Covid-19.

Asian Development Bank (ADB). 2019. Workshop on Tech Start-Ups Support Program in Asia. Held in Seoul, Republic of Korea. 9–12 April.

_____. 2019. *Technical Assistance Report: Digital Development Facility for Asia and the Pacific*. Manila.

P. Astone. 2020. Bailouts for Startups 'Vital for Recovery.' *fDi Intelligence/Financial Times*. 13 May.

British Business Bank. Future Fund: Scheme Overview.

D. David, S. Gopalan, and S. Ramachandran. 2020. The Startup Environment and Funding Activity in India. *ADBI Working Paper Series*. No. 1145. Tokyo: Asian Development Bank Institute.

Enterprise Singapore. 2020. Collated Resources & Support for Startups. 13 April.

Ewing Marion Kauffman Foundation. 2018. *State of Entrepreneurship 2017*. Kansas City. p. 24.

Government of Germany, Federal Ministry for Economic Affairs and Energy. 2020. *Unterstützungspaket für Start-ups.*

Government of Germany, Federal Ministry for Economic Affairs and Energy. 2020. €2 Billion Package of Measures for Start-Ups Finalised. News release. 30 April.

S. Hui Lim. 2020. Policies and Enabling Environment. Insights and Experiences of Enterprise Singapore. Presentation made at the Post-COVID-19 New Normal: Implications for Startup Ecosystems organized by the Asian Development Bank. 4 August.

C. Kaptein. 2020. Driving Financial and Healthcare Inclusion in Emerging Markets. Presented at the Post-COVID-19 New Normal: Implications for Startup Ecosystems organized by the Asian Development Bank. 4 August.

Kreditanstalt für Wiederaufbau (KfW). KfW-Corona-Hilfe: Beteiligungsfinanzierung für Start-ups und kleine Unternehmen.

S. Kuester. 2020. Post-COVID-19 New Normal: Implications for Startup Ecosystems. Presented at the Post-COVID-19 New Normal: Implications for Startup Ecosystems organized by the Asian Development Bank. 4 August.

V. K. Singh. 2020. Policy and Regulatory Changes for a Successful Startup Revolution: Experiences from the Startup Action Plan in India. *ADBI Working Paper series.* No. 1146. Tokyo: Asian Development Bank Institute.

Startup Genome. 2020. *Post-COVID-19 New Normal: Implications for Startup Ecosystems*. Background paper for the Post-COVID-19 New Normal: Implications for Startup Ecosystems organized by the Asian Development Bank. 4 August.

_____. 2020. *The Global Startup Ecosystem Report 2020*.

P. Vandenberg, A. Hampel-Milagrosa, and M. Helble. 2020. Financing of Tech Startups in Selected Asian Countries. *ADBI Working Paper Series.* No. 1115. Tokyo: Asian Development Bank Institute.

Various (crowdsourced document). 2020. *SEAriously Awesome People List – Startup COVID-19 Layoffs*.

An Equity-Focused Digital Strategy for Education during and after COVID-19

Ashish Dhawan
Founder and Chairman
Central Square Foundation

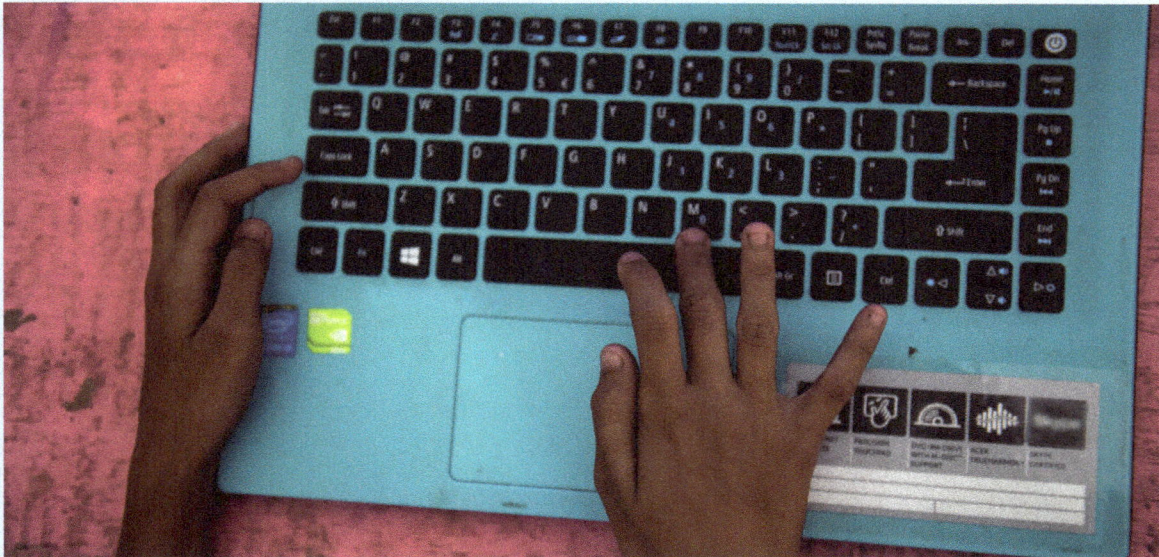

Studying online. Education technology (EdTech) offers a way for students to continue learning while schools are closed, but most EdTech solutions are costly for most parents and school systems.

Introduction

The coronavirus disease (COVID-19) outbreak has prompted countries worldwide to impose mobility restrictions, including temporary cessation of face-to-face schooling. The latest data from the United Nations Educational, Scientific and Cultural Organization (UNESCO) show that around 1 billion students across the globe are affected by the profound disruption to the educational system. Extended school closures could have enormous long-term consequences for today's children, and their learning losses could translate over time into $10 trillion of lost earnings for the global economy.

In India, which has the largest school system in the world, 250 million K-12 students and 10 million teachers have been impacted by school closures. In higher education, 35 million students have been affected. Governments and educational institutions have been pursuing innovative and practical options to cope with the unprecedented situation. While multimodal approaches have been adopted to prevent learning loss, education technology (EdTech) has emerged as a prominent tool for remote learning. Its growth is expected to magnify after the pandemic, with the EdTech market in India projected to reach $1.96 billion.

Although there is no substitute for the in-person learning experience, EdTech holds considerable promise for strengthening educational systems and fostering resilience in future crises. However, it is not a solution by itself nor a one-size-fits-all proposition. Solutions should be aligned with the efforts of central and local governments and different phases of readiness, considering the available infrastructure, platforms, and preparedness of teachers, students, and parents.

Context

India has witnessed notable gains in primary and secondary education, which increased enrollment, retention of students, and the number of schools. The gross enrollment ratio at the elementary level was 91.64% and secondary level 79.6% in 2018–2019. The dropout rates were reduced to 2.72% at the elementary level and 9.74% at the secondary level in the same period.

For higher education, the gross enrollment ratio stands well below the government's target, but has been steadily rising since 2014–2015. Universities and colleges—mostly private—have grown by 37% (universities) and 9% (colleges) over the last 5 years.

The quality of education, however, remains a challenge. Reports show that students are not achieving class-appropriate learning levels. According to the Annual Status of Education Report 2018, over 70% of children in Class 3 cannot do basic reading nor arithmetic. Only 28.1% of children in Class 3 in rural India could do simple subtraction, while 27.2% of them could read a Class 2-level text. In tertiary education, challenges include a shortage of quality faculty, poor pass percentages, and low employability rates among candidates post course completion.

Such problems have been compounded by inequity in technological access. While India has the second-largest internet user base globally with over 718 million subscribers, almost half of its population is not digitally connected.

With movement restrictions to keep the general public safe, online education has served as a viable alternative to face-to-face learning. But students who cannot afford internet connection or are located in remote areas with poor digital infrastructure face difficulties in transitioning to this mode of learning.

Adding to the complexities is the quality of available EdTech solutions. India's EdTech landscape comprises over 4,500 products, but many of these products lack pedagogically sound content. Most of these solutions are also beyond the financial capacity of the majority of parents and school systems and largely cater to students from the high-income group.

Policy Solutions

Collaboration for the development of short-, medium-, and long-term solutions

Educational authorities could benefit from the support and knowledge of stakeholders to determine the appropriate distance learning modalities according to the specific context of their regions. In India, different states demonstrate varying degrees of online education because of infrastructure considerations, the suitability of technology-based learning materials for their students, and digital literacy of users.

Moreover, state governments and educational institutions should forge partnerships with the business sector to provide free or low-cost online courses to learners and teachers, who are likely experiencing increased financial hardship.

Continued multi-stakeholder collaboration in the recovery period will be equally crucial to develop sound strategies for reopening schools and campuses, introduce measures for reversing learning losses, and create a long-term vision for blended learning.

Leveraging existing content and tools for a quick response

With the help of central and state governments, schools and higher educational institutions pivoted to online learning quickly using minimal resources by focusing on existing content and curriculum mapping rather than developing new content. Fortunately, the central government developed the digital architecture before COVID-19, enabling the state governments and their educational systems to rapidly deploy solutions at no cost to learners.

Curation and contextualization of products

With a plethora of EdTech solutions in India, a curated database of free resources was instrumental in helping learners find content that matches their needs. These learning materials needed to be (i) aligned with the curriculum, (ii) translated in local languages for the low-income segment, and (iii) integrated with interactive elements such as gamification to increase engagement. Given the inability of remote learning to replicate the interactions, supervision, and socialization in schools and campuses, solutions should be designed to sustain learners' motivation.

Use of multiple channels

Beyond digital platforms, low-technology and non-technology solutions should be deployed for wider reach. Cognizant of issues with hardware and connectivity among disadvantaged groups, educational authorities in India have used a combination of technologies for multimodal delivery, such as text messaging, radios, and television-based programs. For extremely remote areas or low-resource environments, worksheets are being sent to students' homes for their continued learning.

For digital interventions, more emphasis has been given to asynchronous (on-demand) sessions rather than on synchronous (real-time) classes because of technological limitations for the underprivileged. Lectures are recorded so that they can be viewed later by students who could not get real-time access.

Additional student services

An assessment of students' needs should be conducted to identify any necessary support in this time of crisis and uncertainty. In higher education, there should be measures to assist international or nonlocal students who immediately have to travel back to their home bases. Students on financial aid may also need allowance on devices and internet subscriptions, which are fundamental to their online participation.

Tools and support for parent engagement

As the COVID-19 pandemic has augmented parents' role as teachers, they have been provided with tools necessary for their engagement and involvement in their child's learning activities at home. In addition, teachers' support has been vital for parents who now have to deal with home and work responsibilities concurrently.

Professional development of teachers

Because teachers suddenly need to adapt their pedagogical practices under new circumstances, free platforms have been offered to build their capacities and augment their digital proficiency.

Remote learning is unlikely to fully offset the negative consequences of extended school and campus closures. This highlights the need for continued support and investments in the professional development of teachers whose role will become even more essential in the learning recovery process.

Policy Implementation

Response Phase

Across India

Through multi-stakeholder collaboration, authorities across the country have brought forward measures to facilitate the continuity of education. Recognizing the technological constraints on a sizable portion of the population, policy makers have implemented multichannel responses for accessibility.

Online learning has been made available through Google Meet, Zoom, and other digital platforms. In Delhi, state leadership conducts weekly review sessions with students and teachers, which are livestreamed on YouTube. Similarly, Uttar Pradesh leverages web-based tools to deliver content to teachers and students.

The wide use of WhatsApp has made it an easy and scalable platform for regular communication and learning at home. Networks for parents and teacher professional communities have been created. In Madhya Pradesh, there are approximately 50,000 WhatsApp groups for parents. In Himachal, WhatsApp-based assessment bots measure the learning of children.

With equity as a major consideration for learning initiatives, state governments have supplemented web-based tools with radio and TV-based programs, text messaging, interactive voice response, and non-technology interventions.

Albeit not many, there are also notable efforts for students with disabilities. For example, Uttar Pradesh has created video content for the hearing impaired and audio content for visually impaired learners. Special educators call parents of these children and support parents in using these resources.

At the tertiary level, the University Grants Commission has permitted credit transfer for massive online open courses, allowing students to select courses relevant to them and gain credits. Universities can now also offer their courses for credit to other institutions.

Students

A primary initiative of the Ministry of Human Resource Development, DIKSHA is a repository of engaging e-content to help K-12 students streamline their decision-making and easily find solutions that align with their learning needs. "Energized Textbooks," which are enhanced textbooks with embedded QR codes that allow students to view engaging content in the form of audio and video, are integrated into the DIKSHA platform. Over 80,000 e-books in multiple languages for Classes 1–12 can be accessed on DIKSHA, and the states are printing more than 500 million in the 2020 academic year.

Another interactive K-12 learning resource is TicTacLearn which has content for math and science available in Hindi, English, and regional languages. Available on YouTube and DIKSHA, TicTacLearn provides quality content, engagement, and access—all critical aspects of online learning.

For higher education, the University Grants Commission has created a list of various massive online open courses for dissemination on university websites and social media, outlining the benefits of these courses for students.

Aside from academics, resources have been mobilized to strengthen student services and establish protocols for transparent and regular communications. For example, Ashoka University—a liberal arts university in Haryana—has adopted measures to minimize inconvenience brought by COVID-19 to its students by setting up a help desk, developing a management information system for tracking and resolving all student issues, offering travel assistance, and supporting the needs of students on financial aid.

Parents

Because the pandemic has placed additional teaching responsibilities on parents, they could greatly benefit from the tools to help them manage home-based learning. In India, a first-of-its-kind free mobile app called TopParent enables and empowers parents with the right knowledge, language, and strategies around child development to hone their kids' skills and learning ability.

Additionally, there is an app called Rocket Learning that delivers activity-based content and worksheets to parents on WhatsApp using an automated platform and analyzes students' responses and provides feedback. To keep parents and families engaged in the learning process, the app has group competitions and social media challenges with incentives such as "Smart Family" certifications.

Teachers

Free technologies such as TeacherApp have been leveraged to facilitate progressive conceptual understanding among K-12 teachers through high-quality interactive, digital content. Five state governments—Chhattisgarh, Uttarakhand, Himachal, Uttar Pradesh, and Jharkhand—signed a memorandum of understanding with TeacherApp, which has successfully onboarded over 250,000 teachers to date.

Similarly, free online tools through SWAYAM—a platform initiated by the central government—have been provided to tertiary-level instructors for their professional development.

In terms of instructional design, teachers have switched to an inductive method because live online sessions are not conducive to a traditional teacher-centric approach. Stimulating learners in a virtual setting could be challenging, and inductive pedagogy could be a powerful tool to encourage sharing among students and create engagement. At Ashoka University, for instance, professors provide students with materials for them to study in advance and use real-time lectures for gauging their understanding and discussing ideas. Another technique is using breakout rooms to divide up the class to improve student focus and participation.

Recovery and Resilience Phases

After the crisis, a three-pronged strategy for primary and secondary education could promote wider adoption of EdTech at home and in schools, reinforced by shaping the ecosystem.

Business to consumers (B2C) – Consumers

First, the provision of access and infrastructure coupled with increased parental awareness will be needed for the stronger adoption of EdTech at home. Although there is a significant number of mobile users in India, efforts targeted at isolated students with zero or low technological access will be critical going forward. Unlocking the demand side of parents will hinge on a supply of online products that are pedagogically sound, contextual, and engaging at a reasonable cost.

Business to government (B2G) – Government schools

Second, close collaboration with governments is integral for the sustainable large-scale adoption of EdTech in schools. In light of COVID-19, there is increased state willingness on EdTech, presenting opportunities to support them in developing an EdTech vision and designing a robust school program. Strengthening the procurement capacity and knowledge of governments is paramount to implement EdTech at scale.

Ecosystem building

Lastly, shaping the EdTech ecosystem comes at an opportune time, as many lessons could be drawn from the COVID-19 experience. The crisis has boosted the scope for EdTech and initiatives to make products widely available to the public that could enable better decision-making on which solutions fit their purpose. Reimagining education will also necessitate continued dialogue on policies and reforms for harnessing EdTech.

In higher education, steps for mainstreaming a hybrid approach and lifelong learning should be taken to build a portfolio of expertise and skills in preparation for a knowledge-based economy. With the threat of automation and the permanent impact of COVID-19 on certain types of work, educational systems should be integrated with diverse and digital courses to develop a future-ready workforce and increase individuals' marketability. Creating high-quality asynchronous content and using online coaches for increased student engagement are the key ingredients to scale blended learning at the tertiary level. In India, partnering with research institutions to develop online courses for colleges and universities, which may lack the capacity to do so, may prove useful in realizing this forward-looking strategy.

Recommendations

Equity should be the top consideration

Poorest households will be hit hard by the multiple crises brought by COVID-19. The growing inequity and digital divide underscore the need for accessibility considerations when designing solutions. Policy makers should also include those with disabilities in their COVID-19 responses through investments in technologies that cater to hearing and visually impaired students.

Interventions should be based on different levels of readiness

Policy makers need to focus on what can be done within the current constraints and with available resources. In the interim period, initiatives could be set up immediately using existing infrastructure, basic technology, and diverse channels. For low-resource areas with limited connectivity, options such as SMS, social media-based teaching, and printed materials are best suited for emergency response.

As countries and localities regain their footing in the subsequent phases, interventions can include enhanced tools and technologies to manage continuity and enable better learning experiences.

National and subnational governments have their unique context informing the most sensible interventions in the response and recovery stages. The key tenet is to capitalize on every opportunity in each stage for continuous improvements.

Support should encompass the needs of students, teachers, and parents

Actors in the learning community will need support, not only for academic learning, but also for their social and emotional well-being.

Students should be provided with tools to make remote education engaging for more effective learning. A repository can easily facilitate the discovery of EdTech solutions that best suit their needs to help them make informed decisions.

In higher education, online coaches could help drive student engagement. Systems should be adapted to make digital learning appealing for students through ease of credit transfers and seamless registration with other institutions offering online courses.

For teachers and parents, a key part of their role is to keep learners motivated. They should be provided with guidance on home teaching and means to ask questions or exchange ideas. Setting up parent groups and peer community groups can be a good way to offer pedagogical and socio-emotional support.

Facilitate lifelong learning to prepare for the future of work

Brought to the fore by the unfolding COVID-19 crisis, knowledge economy preparedness demands reforms in educational systems and amplified investments in human capital to future-proof careers. Policy makers have a key role in encouraging lifelong learning by recognizing all forms of education, such as micro-credentials, determining equivalence of formal qualifications, and allowing interinstitutional collaboration to make courses more widely available to different segments of learners in higher education.

Generate evidence on effective remote learning solutions

The spike in the use of EdTech will bring ample data that can be used to track reach, views, and engagement on online platforms. If data can lead to a deeper understanding of what is working so far, the most effective products should be integrated into classroom teaching in the recovery phase. For personalized learning, courses, and micro-credentials targeted at adult learners, evidence on how they translate to work opportunities would enrich the post-pandemic interventions for skills development. Anonymizing the personal data of learners should be strongly considered to safeguard privacy.

Another mechanism to obtain data is through regular calls between teachers, students, and parents. This could help assess the learning behaviors and outcomes, which could inform the educational policies when schools and campuses reopen.

Resources

ASER Centre. 2018. *Annual Status of Education Report (Rural) 2018*. New Delhi.

Ashoka University. 2020. *Ashoka in the Time of COVID-19*.

J. P. Azevedo et al. 2020. *Simulating the Potential Impacts of COVID-19 School Closures on Schooling and Learning Outcomes: A Set of Global Estimates*. Washington, DC: World Bank.

Central Square Foundation. Enabling Home Learning for Children Through EdTech.

_____. 2020. An Equity Focused Digital Strategy for Post COVID World. Presented at ADB's PACER Dialogues. 22 July.

_____. 2020. *Reorienting Education to Mitigate Learning Loss Due to COVID-19 Crisis*. June.

Government of India. 2020. *India Voluntary National Review 2020: Decade of Action: Taking SDGs from Global to Local*. New Delhi.

KPMG, UN Global Compact Network India. 2019. *Enhancing Quality of Education in India by 2030: A F.I.T. Approach to Realising SDG 4*.

Telecom Regulatory Authority of India. 2019. *The Indian Telecom Services: Performance Indicators*.

UNESCO. COVID-19 Impact on Education (accessed 12 August 2020).

University Grants Commission. UGC Advisories/Notices Related to COVID-19 Pandemic.

Policy Lessons from Coursera: Mitigating Education Disruptions and Job Loss

Chad Pasha
Head of APAC for Global Government Partnerships
Coursera

Working online. Industries with highly skilled talent, especially in technology, see higher stock returns and less disruption from COVID-19, while countries that excel in critical skills see lower income inequality.

Introduction

The speed and scale at which the coronavirus disease (COVID-19) pandemic has disrupted education and triggered the loss of jobs are unparalleled. Lockdowns and mobility restrictions to contain the spread of the virus led to the closure of schools and businesses, affecting 1.6 billion learners, as of June 2020 (UNESCO), and 2.7 billion workers or about 81% of the world's workforce, as of April 2020 (ILO).

To help address the challenges, Coursera, one of the world's largest online learning platforms, has launched two pro bono initiatives. One, the Coursera for Campus Response Initiative gives colleges and university students access to most of Coursera's course catalog online at no cost. Two, the Coursera for Workforce Recovery Initiative helps governments provide unemployed workers access to online courses to enable them to gain the knowledge and skills they need for upskilling and reemployment, also at no cost. The response to the initiatives has been remarkable: it raised total enrollments to 10.3 million in 30 days, up by 644% in April 2020 from April 2019, and increased new user enrollments by 15%.

The enormous demand and appetite for online learning highlighted by Coursera's experience provide a strong basis for escalating the use of digital technologies to support education and learning outcomes amid the pandemic and beyond. Building on the momentum created by the initiatives, public and private stakeholders can maximize the benefits of these technologies by expanding the possibilities for making them accessible to everyone.

Strategic Challenges and COVID-19 Impacts

Even prior to COVID-19, strategic workforce development issues have already confronted governments from both developed and developing economies. Labor markets worldwide are undergoing radical changes as automation gains ground in several industries.

Within the next decade, some 1.1 billion jobs will be radically transformed, 300 million people will be entering the workforce, and the demand for advanced information technology and programming skills will rise by 90%. These changes imply difficult transitions for millions of workers and the need for proactive investment in developing agile learners and skilled talent.

COVID-19 has accelerated the need for workers to become part of the digital shift as the world of work becomes increasingly automated. Disproportionately impacting low-skilled workers, it has also exposed disparities in the employability of workers. These disparities stem from inequalities in access to education and skills development, which could aggravate in a post-COVID world if left unattended.

Key insights gathered from Coursera's platform data in the last 12 months may help stakeholders better understand the pandemic's impacts on the skills and education landscape and how best to move forward.

Countries with higher labor force participation rates are also those with higher skill proficiencies. Skills are essential to quality and sustainable employment. Correspondingly, the higher the skills and skill proficiencies of a country, the higher labor participation is in the job market. The loss of 435 million jobs in the first half of 2020 (UNESCO), mostly in the informal sector and among low-wage workers, is associated with these groups' lack of skills and skill proficiencies.

Industries with more highly skilled talent, especially in technology, see higher stock returns and less disruption from COVID-19. The stock performance of companies is positively correlated to their skill proficiencies. The correlation between an industry's skill proficiency and its stock return in the United States (US) in 2020 is 43% across all domains: 39% for technology, 30% for business, and 21% for data science skill proficiencies. From April to June 2020, the correlation is 40%, suggesting that companies with higher skill proficiency have seen their valuation disrupted less by COVID-19. With the sudden push to remote work, digital skills have also been essential to helping companies respond to the crisis.

Countries that excel in critical skills see lower income inequality. With labor markets thrown into turmoil by COVID-19 and technology putting large populations at risk of losing their jobs, countries should consider the impact of their skills landscape on income inequality. Coursera data reveal a negative correlation between a country's average skill proficiency across domains and the fraction of income held by the top 10% of its population. In the US, the share of income held by the top 10% of its population is 31%, and its average skill proficiency is 58%. In contrast, the share of income held by the top 10% population in Canada is 25%, and its average skill proficiency is 71%.

Online learning is a viable means for people to continue their education amid COVID-19. The massive shift to online learning, indicated by the huge spike in total enrollments after Coursera launched its two initiatives, reflects people's need as well as interest to continue learning amid the pandemic. Huge surges were seen in all the Coursera learning domains.

Design and Implementation

Coursera works through two initiatives to respond to COVID-19 impacts.

Coursera Campus Response Initiative. Launched on 12 March 2020, this initiative is designed for university and college faculty and administrators who need to move their curriculum online and serve many students or an entire campus amid the widespread national and localized school closures. Universities and colleges can sign up to provide their enrolled students access to about 4,000 courses, 400 specializations, and 500 guided projects from Coursera's university and industry partners. Content spans business, data science, computer science, health, information technology, social sciences, arts and humanities, and more.

Participating universities and colleges are given 5,000 licenses each and have access to Coursera's course catalog for free until 30 October 2020. The catalog includes content from university and industry partners. Students who enroll on or before 30 October 2020 will continue to have access to their course for at least 2 months from the date of enrollment. Certificates will be awarded by the universities where the students enroll and complete their courses.

Coursera Workforce Recovery Initiative. Started on 24 April 2020, this initiative enables governments to offer high-quality, job-relevant online learning to workers who lost their jobs amid the pandemic and other unemployed people. The mechanics for joining are the same as those of the Coursera for campuses, but the learning content has been curated to align workers' reskilling and upskilling to both industry demand and workers' needs.

Under the initiative, the unemployed can learn content related to job readiness, displaced workers' retraining, entrepreneurship, "bridge" to post-secondary training, "macro" digital literacy, and job search self-care. These learning modules enable them to go from zero education entry-level to completing 4-month courses and getting jobs in high demand. A course certificate is issued for each completed course.

Participating governments are given 50,000 licenses each and until 30 October 2020 to enroll their unemployed workers. Enrolled learners can continue to have access to finish their courses until 31 December 2020. Large nonprofit or nongovernment organizations dedicated to providing services to unemployed workers may be considered on a case-to-case basis.

Customized features. User-customized features to enhance the quality, effectiveness, relevance, and usability of the online learning experience have been incorporated into the design of the initiatives. Renowned professors providing bite-size video lessons, applied projects, interactive quizzes, and peer-reviewed assignments keep students learning under the Coursera for campuses. The engagement of top universities and industry-leading companies in the workforce recovery courses and specializations ensures world-class content. Learning content for both initiatives is also available anytime, anywhere in multiple languages, and it is simple to launch and manage apps.

Outcomes

User response to these online learning initiatives has been remarkable.

Coursera for Campus Response Initiative. Universities have responded to this initiative only a couple of weeks after it was launched. In Southeast Asia, 156 universities have signed up, 47 of which are from Indonesia, 28 from the Philippines, 24 from Myanmar, 23 from Thailand, 18 from Malaysia, 8 from Singapore, 5 from Viet Nam, and 3 from Cambodia. Some 1.4 million students worldwide have enrolled in over 8 million different courses and counting.

Recognizing that COVID-19 will not go away anytime soon, universities worldwide are also taking a long-term view. Many have signed partnerships with Coursera and other online providers for 2 to 3 years to ensure sustained delivery of blended and online learning. Most of these partnerships are with universities from the US, Europe, South Asia, East Asia, and Australia. The longer-term partnerships provide greater scope to invest in local language customization and private authoring.

Coursera for Workforce Recovery Initiative. More than 250 contracts with government agencies at national, regional, state, and city levels in over 90 countries have been signed within about 2 months after this initiative was launched. Participating countries in Asia and the Pacific include Australia, Bhutan, India, Kazakhstan, Malaysia, Pakistan, the Philippines, and Singapore. Globally, some 200,000 learners have enrolled, and 3.8 million licenses have been requested.

Malaysia is among those granted the largest number of licenses with about 10,000 enrollees. Many enrollees have already completed their courses and received certificates and are currently looking for jobs.

The thousands of learners in data science, cybersecurity, and Python content from the Philippines have an 88% completion rate with a customer satisfaction rating or net promoter score of 71. The learning content in the Philippines reflects the retraining needs of workers, as artificial intelligence begins to displace jobs in the business processing outsourcing sector.

In Singapore, thousands of government officials are trained in data science, computer science, and leadership.

Lessons

The massive displacement of lower-skilled, lower-wage workers precipitated by the COVID-19 pandemic joltingly reminds public and private stakeholders as well as educational institutions of the urgent need to accelerate the pursuit of policy and program measures to reduce the vulnerability of workers to sudden economic downturns. Efforts to reduce this vulnerability must build on the existing field realities, but also address upcoming challenges. Coursera's experience in helping reduce such vulnerability through online learning may provide insights on the best way forward.

Overall, trends in higher education are supportive of escalating blended learning and using digital technologies to achieve sustainable development outcomes. The quick and positive response received by Coursera to its Campus Response Initiative has revealed the readiness of many higher education institutions to maximize the use of blended learning and digital approaches in meeting their educational objectives. In many universities, professors have preferred to deliver content through videos and digital means rather than face-to-face lectures and tutorials. Learning content and delivery are also becoming more modular and stackable to allow for a self-paced and individualized learning approach. Alignment of online content to industry needs and acceptance of credentials by governments need to be strengthened in the face of these trends for countries to ensure that online learning is in line with and supportive of their education goals.

While formal education remains vital, lifelong learning at work is also critical to enabling workforces to adapt to the rapid technological and economic changes affecting the world of work. It has become most pressing for governments to bring together all the key players, including companies, industry associations, and organized labor, to craft short- to medium- and long-term workforce recovery solutions. Efforts to reskill and upskill workers must intensify, and so should enhancements in existing labor-related educational programs.

Workforce development is challenging without reliable data, adequate government resources, and common benchmarks. Outdated, inaccurate, and patchy unemployment and skills records in several countries have made Coursera's work in determining the most feasible job paths and course content for its workforce recovery learners more challenging. Similarly, the lack of government resources and capacity to run large-scale programs have hampered the reach and localization of its services. But solutions have come about for some of these challenges.

Malaysia's social media campaigns to get updated information on its unemployed citizens have enabled it to include many of them in Coursera's Workforce Recovery Initiative. Using simple and low-cost platforms to engage and monitor learners, inviting interns and apprentices to assist, and mobilizing community-based agencies and trained volunteers to do pro bono content translations have helped offset the lack of government resources.

Replicating these sample solutions while building a comprehensive, updated unemployment and skills database will support the development and sustained pursuit of workforce development strategies targeting the most vulnerable sectors. Coursera will contribute to accelerating these processes by making more local language content available in its online learning modules and refining the metrics for measuring success in workforce recovery. Moreover, it explored funding and sponsorship models, engaging multilateral organizations and the private sector, to support governments' continued participation in the Workforce Recovery Initiative when their licenses expired in December 2020.

Employability has become increasingly dependent on stronger tech and data skills. Asian economies are among the largest in the world. Yet, according to Coursera's Global Skills Index 2020, Asian countries are largely missing from the top 20 most skilled nations. The region's overall tech and data science skills are lagging, with major skills deficits in math, statistical programming, and software engineering.

The lack of tech and data science skills across the region can be attributed partly to poor-quality science, technology, engineering, and mathematics education in many countries, which struggle to equip students with essential employment skills. The need for stronger science, technology, engineering, and mathematics programs is heightened by the region's brain drain, reducing the supply of skilled workers locally.

This challenge needs to be addressed by countries across the region. Without considerable investment in upskilling the workforce, many Asian workers will be devastated by the Fourth Industrial Revolution and the pandemic's pervasive impact.

Resources

J. Bughin et al. 2018. *Skill Shift: Automation and the Future of the Workforce*. McKinsey Global Institute.

Coursera. *Global Skills Index 2020* (accessed 12 August 2020).

P. Daugherty, B. Ghosh, and J. Wilson. 2020. *Your Legacy or Your Legend? A CEO's Guide to Getting the Most Out of New Technologies*. Accenture.

International Labour Organization (ILO). 2020. *ILO: As Job Losses Escalate, Nearly Half of Global Workforce at Risk of Losing Livelihoods*. Press release. 29 April.

_____. 2020. *ILO Monitor: COVID-19 and the World of Work. 3rd edition*. Briefing note. 29 April.

J. O'Leary, C. Widener, and S. Agarwal. 2018. *Closing the Talent Gap: Five Ways Government and Business Can Team Up to Reskill Workers*. Deloitte Center for Government Insights.

C. Pasha. 2020. Empowering Higher Education and Workforce Development with Digital Technology. Presented at ADB's PACER Dialogues. 22 July.

World Economic Forum. 2020. *Jobs of Tomorrow: Mapping Opportunity in the New Economy. Geneva*. 22 January.

CHAPTER 4
Reigniting Southeast Asia and Bouncing Back Stronger Together

Harmonizing Health Standards for Post-Quarantine COVID-19 Settings

Jeremy Lim
Co-Director of Global Health, Saw Swee Hock School of Public Health
National University of Singapore

Social distancing in a food court. A food court in Singapore marks seats to be left empty to ensure safe distancing between customers.

Introduction

Since its emergence in late 2019, the coronavirus disease (COVID-19) pandemic has spread to 188 countries with millions infected and dead, and the numbers continue to rise daily.[7]

The disease is caused by severe acute respiratory syndrome coronavirus (SARS-CoV)-2, a novel pathogen from a large family of coronaviruses that have caused epidemics in the past. Unlike its predecessor, which was responsible for SARS in 2003, SARS-CoV-2 is more contagious and manifests itself in much broader clinical spectrums, ranging from asymptomatic presentation to severe pneumonia and death. Coupled with other factors such as our increased global interconnectedness and lack of effective treatments, this has contributed to the rapid spread of the virus and poses a challenge of unprecedented scale.

---

[7] The Johns Hopkins University. COVID-19 Dashboard by the Center for Systems Science and Engineering (CSSE) at Johns Hopkins (accessed 1 July 2020).

Although vaccines have been fast-tracked, efforts to roll out vaccines may be further delayed by regulatory hurdles, liability concerns, manufacturing issues, and the lack of robust data. Public health (non-pharmaceutical) interventions are, therefore, important to reduce the caseload until such a time that a substantial portion of the population is vaccinated to achieve herd immunity.

Public health interventions are typically deployed across societies at varying points of the virus transmission pathway network. The goal is to flatten the infection curve to prevent overloading health systems by slowing transmission and spreading case incidents over a longer period. This is conceptually framed by our understanding of R0, the basic reproduction number, estimated to be between 2 and 3 for COVID-19.[8] By bringing this number down, governments may reduce the epidemic's intensity, thus taking pressure off health systems.

However, epidemic control measures come with attendant societal and economic costs, and the more rigorous the public health measures, the larger the nonpublic health costs. Closing off borders dampens trade, shutting down cities upends businesses, etc.—all of which are expected to cost the global economy $1 trillion in 2020.[9] As Nobel Laureate economist Robert Shiller puts it, there are dual contagions at play here—a massive health contagion and a parallel contagion of severe economic distress. "Lives or livelihoods" is a false dichotomy; it's "lives and livelihoods."

What then is in the menu of options for policy makers to consider, and when should policy makers deploy which interventions? What are the minimum measures to be retained when adjusting for economic disruptions? We take a look at the main interventions available, the economic and health considerations surrounding them, and discuss how this balancing act might play out in real life.

Policy Options

Epidemic control measures are usually built around key points in the virus's transmission pathways, forming three key layers of defense against the spread of the disease (Table 4.1).

Border controls seek to prevent the importation of the virus into the country, while active and general measures are deployed to reduce community transmissions once imported cases have been "seeded" within national borders. All three layers of defense involve some form of "safe distancing," a term encompassing a broad set of measures aimed at reducing physical interactions on individual, community, and population levels to prevent human transmissions. A point to note here is that the term "social distancing" is less preferred as the social elements of interaction are important for mental health and should be preserved wherever possible. It should be emphasized that these interventions are a suite and are not mutually exclusive. They work best when deployed together.

---

8   A. Tan. 2020. Everyone Has Part to Play to Flatten Epidemic Curve: Expert. *The Straits Times*. 24 March.

9   *World Economic Forum*. 2020. This Is How Much the Coronavirus Will Cost the World's Economy, according to the UN. 17 March.

Table 4.1: Epidemic Control Measures for a Post-Lockdown Period

Measures			Examples
Border controls	From source area, which may be extended over time		From Wuhan, then Hubei; closure of the Victoria, New South Wales border in Australia
	From source country (outside source area, but administratively easily delineable)		From the whole of the People's Republic of China
	From other countries or areas from which there have been incidences of infections		Visa suspension for select nationalities
Active measures to identify and isolate cases and close contacts	Detection of potential cases	Imported potential cases	Through screening at health-care (and other) facilities
		Suspected unlinked confirmed cases	
		Contacts of confirmed imported cases	By contact tracing
	Isolation or quarantine	Health-care facilities (hospitals)	Hospital infection control, protection of health-care personnel
		Homes	
		Quarantine facilities	
	Treatment, including financial support for treatment costs and loss of income		With Remdesivir, Ritonavi or Lopinavir
	Release		Release after ascertainment of non-infectiousness
General measures (community measures, mitigating measures, etc.)	Measures to reduce contact within the community (social or safe distancing)		Reducing public gatherings, school and business closures
	Public communications		Community sanitation and hygiene, mask use, self-isolation if unwell
	Provision of necessities and other supplies		Masks, medical, and food supplies
	Others		Environmental cleansing, business continuity planning, etc.

Source: National University of Singapore, Saw Swee Hock School of Public Health. 2020. COVID-19 Science Report: Containment Measures.

There is a high degree of variation in the exact implementation (extent, scale, and duration) of public health interventions, with varying results as well. New Zealand's tiered lockdown of 77 days managed to completely "eliminate" the virus. In India, daily case numbers continue to climb despite stringent controls that commenced in late March. Taipei,China went without a lockdown, but still managed to control its disease situation effectively; success factors include quick preparation and early intervention. The United Kingdom infamously attempted a herd immunity strategy during the outbreak's early stages, triggering widespread backlash and an eventual reversal in policy.

This lack of harmonization in policy-making is largely inevitable. SARS-CoV-2 emerged and spread with such rapidity that many governments resorted to implementing a cascade of changing, ad hoc interventions, which continue to play out even as countries begin to lift restrictions. Different countries also have vastly different resources with very different transmission and sociopolitical contexts, driving the practical implementation and lifting of restrictions. There is no playbook to follow, and every country has to "cross the river by feeling the stones," as former Chinese leader Deng Xiaoping said.

A middle ground thus has to be reached. Globally coordinated standards and principles could be maintained, promulgated, and evolved in the light of new evidence while allowing room for countries to consider and adapt guidance dynamically. The World Health Organization (WHO) has already published some general guidance for containing the current health contagion. We would do well to incorporate socioeconomic factors for a more nuanced balancing of lives and livelihoods.

Objectives, Considerations, and Approaches

There are four objectives to achieve in these difficult situations. First, to test, trace, and isolate cases as soon as possible to avoid secondary cases and widespread community transmission. Second, to prevent hospital and health system resources from being overwhelmed. Third, to enable cautious economic reopening so that livelihoods can be maintained. And lastly, to prepare citizens and businesses for the profound changes that a COVID-19 world necessitates.

Balancing these four objectives will be dynamic, requiring multidisciplinary decision-making and access to real-time information. A key need is a better understanding of risk. There is no threshold of zero risks. The probabilistic risks of business activities versus health system capacity to cope with a surge in cases should be used in decision-making. There is no ex ante right or wrong here. Officials across health and economic agencies should openly debate options.

Regular severity monitoring and risk assessments will be critical to informing policy-making and actions to be taken at each threat level. For one, there is useful, albeit dynamic data emerging from the US about the risks of various business activities across 100 well-known occupations.[10] These were derived via an evaluation of three physical attributes: contact with others, level of physical proximity, and exposure to disease and infection. Public officials, who can be selective in the activities and businesses to be permitted, should study these carefully when calibrating lockdowns or unlocking measures.

Critical enablers to a successful COVID-19 internal response—and subsequently, a less dangerous reopening—will involve the fulfillment of various stakeholder roles on the part of health agencies, the rest of the government, and the public. On the clinical front, health agencies must test, trace, and isolate cases aggressively and preserve health system capacity. The rest of the government will have to augment their work, ensure strong enforcement and supply chain effectiveness, and maintain sound communications and public trust. Economic rescue packages will be critical to support livelihoods and foster cooperation with public health measures. On the side of the public, strong digital enablement and an understanding and willingness to sacrifice for a greater good seem to correlate highly with a country's success.

---

[10]   M. Lu. 2020. The Front Line: Visualizing the Occupations with the Highest COVID-19 Risk. *Visual Capitalist*. 15 April.

We posit that a recurring loop of risk assessments, early detection of outbreaks, and micro-lockdowns will define the "next normal"—analogous to a game of whack-a-mole. We have already seen this in the People's Republic of China, the Republic of Korea, and most recently, Australia. It is important to keep in mind that countries unlock not because they are out of the woods, but because the economic consequences of safe distancing are too damaging and unacceptable to the public.

Countries will have to define the acceptable levels of risks in relation to economic implications and continuously implement and relax public health interventions depending on the outbreak situation. Business and municipal disruptions will form a recurring theme—both will have to reinvent. Businesses may switch to "tele-everything" structures with greater emphasis on e-commerce. Neighborhoods and cities may evolve in tandem to become more self-contained and greener.

We have provided here a stepladder approach based on resource availability to what we deem as minimum measures for a post-lockdown period for policy makers to consider (Table 4.2). As aforementioned, there is no single formula for all, and careful consideration is needed based on a country's capacity and infrastructure. That said, public health measures such as wearing masks and handwashing or sanitizing are safe, inexpensive, and incur minimal inconvenience, and as such should be widely adopted.

Table 4.2: Minimum Measures for a Post-Lockdown Period

#	Measure	Level
1	Mandate mask use, basic hand hygiene and etiquette	LEVEL 1
1	Safe distancing advisories	LEVEL 1
1	Health education (symptoms, mode of transmission)	LEVEL 1
1	International border restrictions	LEVEL 1
1	Increase ventilation in public spaces	LEVEL 1
1	Cancel or adapt mass gatherings	LEVEL 1
2	Provide materials for basic hand hygiene	LEVEL 2
2	Close nonessential businesses	LEVEL 2
2	Schools: rotate in attendance, temporary closures	LEVEL 2
2	Simple manual contact tracing	LEVEL 2
2	Staggered shifts, flexible leave policies for workers	LEVEL 2
2	Teleconsultations	LEVEL 2
3	Antimicrobial coating on high-touch surface areas	LEVEL 3
3	Recruitment of safe distancing enforcement officers	LEVEL 3
3	Increase testing and screening capacity	LEVEL 3
3	Increase health care and support	LEVEL 3
3	Set up more remote medical centers, quarantine areas	LEVEL 3
3	Increase social and financial support	LEVEL 3
4	Authorities can provide masks to all citizens	LEVEL 4
4	Enhanced contact tracing	LEVEL 4
4	Engage digital ambassadors to increase digital literacy	LEVEL 4
4	Work-from-home, home-based learning schemes	LEVEL 4
4	Enhanced psychological protection	LEVEL 4
4	Support medical research and advancements	LEVEL 4

Source: Author.

A final word on cross-border movements—there is a tremendous opportunity and need for countries to work together to harmonize inbound and outbound travel protocols and standards. The European Union has already begun to lift nonessential travel restrictions on 14 "safe" countries; decision factors include the country's epidemiological situation, reciprocity, and reliability of national data.[16] "Fast lane" arrangements with multiple preconditions (e.g., pre-departure and post-arrival health measures, controlled itineraries) are also being trialed across countries and municipalities. Moving forward, countries may consider developing central registries for test results, interoperable digital trackers, and standardized lab techniques to facilitate such movements better.

Resource

J Lim. 2020. Minimum Public Health Interventions for Post COVID-19 Lockdown: Lives and Livelihoods. Presented at ADB's PACER Dialogues. 1 July.

Adaptive Control of COVID-19 Outbreaks: Policy Approaches

Anup Malani
Professor
University of Chicago

Social distancing street markings. White circles were drawn on a road in India to enforce social distancing (photo by iStock/Abhishek Kumar Sah).

Introduction

The coronavirus disease (COVID-19) pandemic has compelled government authorities to design and implement policy responses in a rapidly evolving situation. Many countries have introduced containment strategies of varying degrees and duration. Some have begun relaxing these measures, while others are reinstating restrictive policies as they experience a resurgence.

Epidemic control policies come with social and economic consequences. Thus, there is hesitation over what minimum measures should be retained, what measures can be eased, and in what sequence to pave the way for cautious economic reopening.

The unpredictability of the COVID-19 trajectory leads to ambiguity around the optimal policy regime for managing and controlling infection and progressively allowing economic activities. Nearly all governments, including those in Southeast Asia, face this immense challenge.

Recent experience in India highlights the need for COVID-19 forecasting models to guide suppression policies. Suppression through an adaptive control strategy could allow countries, states, or cities to bring infection rates under control while allowing modest levels of economic activity. A modeling framework could also be instrumental for targeting supplies of an eventual vaccine, which will be quite limited in the initial stages of introduction.

Challenges

The crisis has forced governments to confront multifaceted challenges with completely new policy-making approaches under conditions of uncertainty. Governments have pursued policies with limited information and inadequate consideration and analysis of the benefits and trade-offs of different containment measures.

When the World Health Organization (WHO) declared COVID-19 as a pandemic, several countries imposed lockdown measures to stem the spread of the virus. However, most of these nations—especially those with inadequate resources—cannot afford to sustain extreme restrictions that are crippling their economies.

Another issue that has complicated matters for governments is the lag between when policies are enacted and when they affect the disease, as well as a lag between dates of infection and death. Looking at current infections or deaths for policy-making can lead to errors. One may underestimate or overestimate the cases occurring when the policy finally has an impact on cases. Instead, governments should generate forecasts to determine what changes need to be made today.

Key Considerations

Countries have different sociopolitical contexts, health systems, resources, and epidemiological challenges. Thus, their containment strategies should be targeted and localized. More importantly, they need to pursue evidence-based frameworks during this pandemic to better enact policies that improve health outcomes while reducing economic burdens. As such, accurate and timely data are fundamental to strengthening policy measures, especially in a situation such as the COVID-19 crisis that requires science-based and targeted responses with due consideration for both immediate and long-term consequences.

Whether the pandemic severity is high, medium, or low in a given location, testing remains critical to obtain the necessary data for detecting cases and isolating patients. There is a tendency to test symptomatic individuals mainly, but asymptomatic carriers must also be identified to minimize the chain of transmission.

Crucially, timely reporting of these tests ensures that data is up-to-date. This is critical for generating reliable forecasts to identify emerging hot spots and make policy refinements according to changing local conditions.

Along with virological testing, serological testing can provide a vital piece of the puzzle for policy-making in the context of COVID-19. This type of test shows evidence of past exposure and infection, helping determine the level of immunity in a population. Such information helps authorities assess the vulnerability of a particular community and will prove valuable for allocating the constrained supplies of COVID-19 vaccine.

Adaptive Control for Suppression Policies

As more countries build their domestic capacity for testing, they become armed with more data that could help them predict the course of COVID-19 and integrate adaptive control into their policy responses.

Adaptive control is a flexible countercyclical policy approach, whereby different areas release from lockdown in potentially different gradual ways, depending on the local progression of the disease. It requires flexibility to decrease or increase social distancing in response to observed and projected dynamics of the outbreak. Adaptive control has three basic principles. First, **suppression policy should have a clear epidemiological target or objective**. For example, a target may be related to lowering the reproductive rate (Rt), which refers to transmissibility. Setting a target on Rt captures the need to control the momentum of the infection.

Alternatively, an objective could be focused on keeping the trajectory of deaths low or ensuring adequate health-care capacity, such as the ratio of hospital beds to hospitalizations. The focus on deaths overcomes the problem that the number of cases is a function of testing policy, which may in practice be inadequate.

When setting targets, policy makers should account for incentives to manipulate data. If the target is associated with the level of COVID-19 cases, there might be an inclination to conceal true data for fear of a lockdown. Therefore, it is recommended to combine objectives with a testing rate requirement to ensure data integrity.

The second principle is to **measure targets locally and periodically** since Rt can vary across locations and change over time. Regular monitoring at the local level allows policy makers to recalibrate policy responses based on recent data from a particular community.

The third principle is to **map targets to suppression policies**. For instance, if Rt is below 1, which is considered an optimal level of transmissibility, restrictions and social distancing policies could be relaxed or lifted accordingly (Table 4.3). An Rt above 2 warrants extreme policies on mobility to curb the outbreak.

Table 4.3: COVID-19 Restrictions Based on the Transmissibility Level

Target/Trigger	Social Distancing Policy
$2 \leq Rt$	Maximum lockdown observed
$1.5 \leq Rt < 2$	2/3 to maximum amount of lockdown
$1 \leq Rt < 1.5$	1/3 to maximum amount of lockdown
$Rt < 1$	Minimum lockdown, voluntary social distancing

COVID-19 = coronavirus disease, Rt = reproductive rate.
Source: Author.

Forecasting for Vaccination Policies

While there are global initiatives such as the COVID-19 Vaccines Global Access (COVAX) to ensure equitable access to supplies, these do not offer a framework for within-country distribution policy. To address this issue, the government should devise the vaccination target using forecast modeling of Rt and serological studies. By identifying a portion of the population with prior infection, policy makers could account for individuals with acquired immunity in their targets. Testing for T cells, instead of antibodies, is strongly recommended as it is better suited for detecting immunity.

It is important to note that the level of vaccine efficacy based on clinical studies should be factored into the calculation of targets. Thus, a lower efficacy would lead to a higher target. Distribution policy should also be localized as risks and herd immunity threshold vary by location. Since the rate of a population's exposure to COVID-19 increases over time, serological testing should be done close to the date of vaccination. While there are uncertainties on when a vaccine becomes available and when it could be administered, surveillance is a feasible approach that could be done repeatedly to assess the incidence of infection.

Moreover, distribution policy should be reflective of the main goal of vaccination. When a goal is centered on health, vaccine prioritization should account for individual-level attributes that are easy to identify, such as age, gender, occupation, etc., to implement a model at scale. Based on individual-level data, estimates on Rt, probability of infections, and deaths per category can be determined, thereby allowing an evidence-based priority allocation methodology for vaccination.

Policy Implementation

India's experience has shown that a gradual and localized approach allows for safer reopening and reduced infection rates.

A strategy was developed using adaptive control to inform state policy in India with three main parts: (i) gradual introduction of activities, (ii) setting and tracking epidemiological targets such as reducing the Rt below 1 and adjusting social distancing every week or two to meet those targets, and (iii) adoption of different policies in different districts or cities based on local conditions.

An execution plan was also devised with four steps: (i) identifying gaps in existing data and decision-analysis tools, (ii) gathering more comprehensive COVID-related data to fill gaps in existing data, (iii) building evidence-based models of epidemiological outcomes and economic activity to address gaps in existing decision analysis tools, and (iv) leveraging the epidemiological and economic outcomes to extract actionable recommendations from data.

On 24 March 2020, India announced a nationwide lockdown—known as Lockdown 1.0—one of the most severe shutdowns worldwide. On 21 April 2020, the government announced Lockdown 2.0, which allowed some states to relax controls in certain places. Adaptive control and Lockdown 3.0 commenced in early May 2020, introducing the idea of a zoned shutdown and calibrating policies according to local risk.

The Ministry of Home Affairs, with assistance from the Ministry of Health and Family Welfare, issued an order that classifies districts across India based on their recent case counts (Table 4.4).

Table 4.4: Classification of Districts Based on Case Counts

Zone Category	Pandemic Severity
Red	Sizable number of cases detected, or areas declared as hot spots
Orange/Yellow	Few cases found with no increase in the number of infections
Green	No confirmed cases in the last 21 days

Source: Ministry of Home Affairs and Ministry of Health and Family Welfare, India.

Green zones were allowed to begin all activities except air and interstate bus and rail transport, and the opening of schools, hotels, malls, etc., while red zones were required to maintain stringent limitations. All other districts were classified as orange and yellow zones, limiting local taxis and local bus capacity. Within each of these color-coded zones, states may establish "containment zones" as small as a building, floor, or even a home, which would be subject to even more severe restrictions than red zones.

Zone classification with the corresponding Rt determined the kind of restrictions placed on the movement of people and supply of goods in a district (Table 4.5). Red was for full lockdown or no release, orange for 1/3 step toward full release, yellow for 2/3 step toward full release, and green for a full release. On 17 May 2020, the Ministry of Home Affairs announced Lockdown 4.0, which allowed states to determine which districts fall under a zone category. This enabled local authorities to balance local infection risk against local economic impact. Lockdown 5.0 on 8 June 2020 allowed a phased economic reopening of all areas outside the containment zones.

Table 4.5: Restrictions Based on Zone Classification

Rt	Zone	Policy/Release	Travel to/from Other Districts
$2 \leq Rt$	Red	None	None
$1.5 \leq Rt < 2$	Orange	1/3	None
$1 \leq Rt < 1.5$	Yellow	2/3	None
$Rt < 1$	Green	Full	Only other green districts in the state

Rt = reproductive rate.
Source: Author.

Outcomes

Simulations based on the susceptible-infected-recovered model show that adaptive control allows states in India to contain their infection rates while facilitating modest levels of economic functions.

In Bihar, which is the third-largest state and home to 100 million people, projections on the number of cases per district with policy simulations were conducted every 2–3 weeks. Authorities coordinated with local officials based on the information provided, including emerging "hot" regions or where infections are growing rapidly, to determine which districts had to tighten controls.

Dialogue with officials also provided an opportunity to offer guidance on best practices, including controlling the spread of the virus with labor migration and conducting serological testing with limited resources and capacity.

Figure 4.1 shows the simulations in Bihar, suggesting that adaptive control does better than either an immediate release from lockdown on 12 September 2020 or delay by another week. As illustrated, there is an initial increase in cases with adaptive control, but a reduction is expected to occur over time and within a shorter duration.

Figure 4.1: Simulations in Bihar State

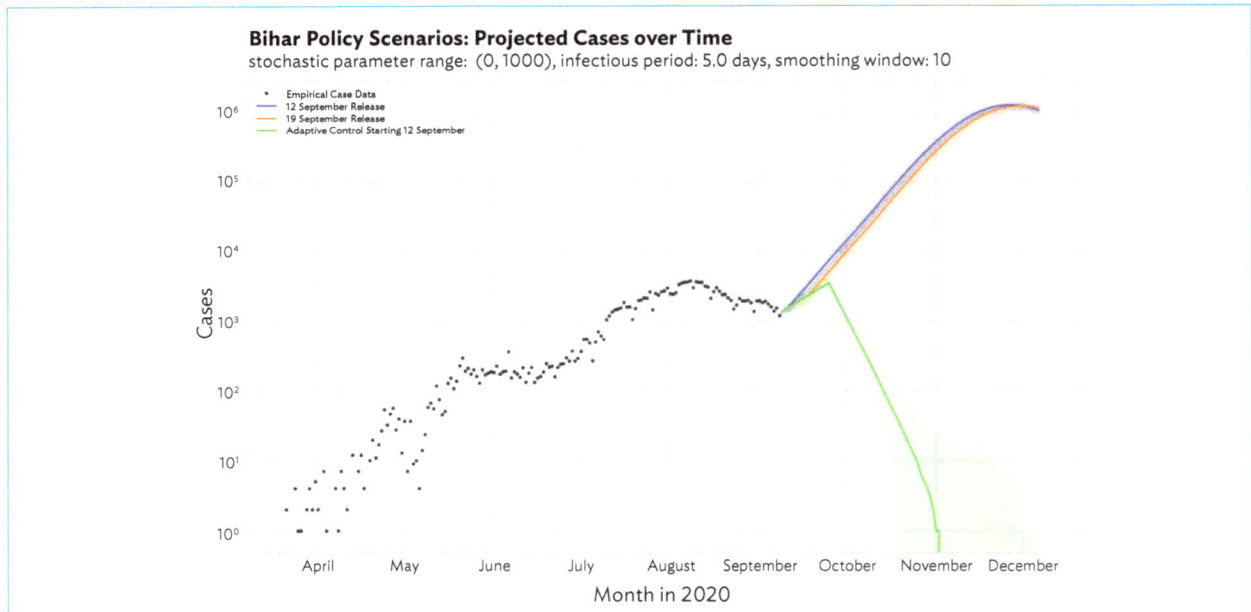

Source: Author.

Similar work is being done across Indonesia. Forecasting is coupled with capacity building to enable local ministries and researchers to develop models themselves, and to make their data management more robust by enhancing their knowledge to spot data anomalies to make the necessary corrections in their models.

In Jakarta, simulations show a more positive scenario with adaptive control than immediate release and extended lockdown (Figure 4.2).

Figure 4.2: Simulations in Jakarta, Indonesia

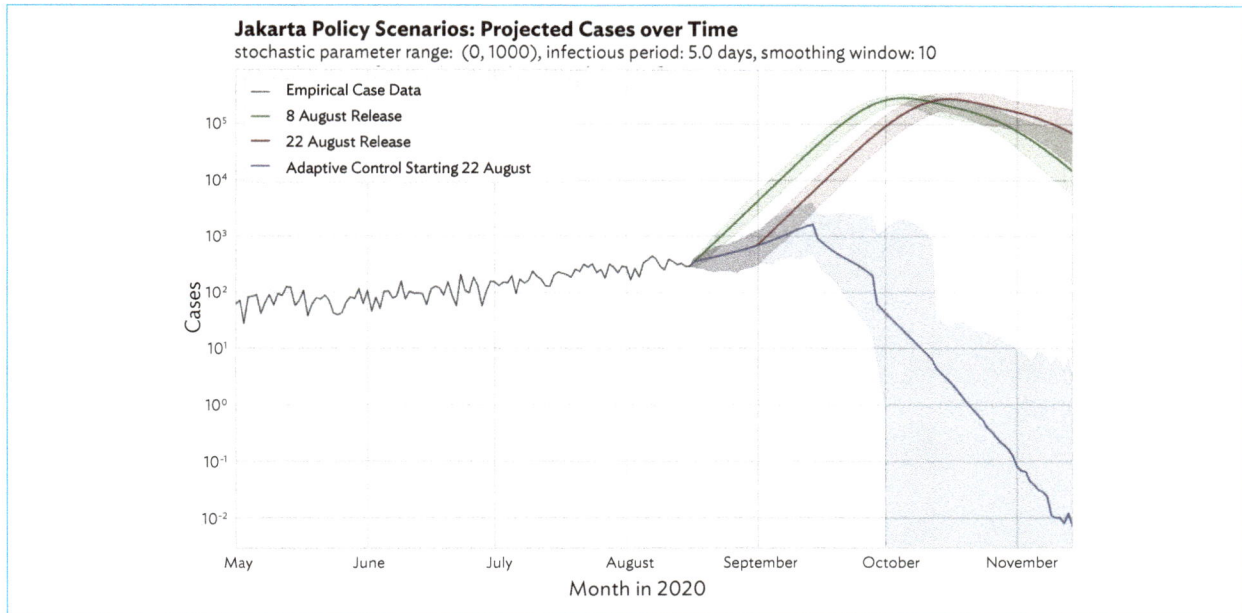

Source: Author.

Recommendations

Expanding testing is critical

While countries await more COVID-19 vaccines, testing on a larger scale would be required to reopen economies gradually. This enables a better understanding of epidemiology as well as strategic planning for future health-care needs.

In addition to testing for the virus, serological testing—which provides data on immunity—will be useful to inform a local community's vaccination distribution policy. Since immunity levels change over time, it is important for serological testing to be done as close as possible to the date of vaccination.

Due to selection in testing and latency in reporting, it is important to correct any flaws in data. A sound data science approach accounts for uncertainties in predictions, and a model should be constantly recalibrated as new data become available.

Continuously reevaluate containment strategies and take account of health and economic consequences

As lockdown fatigue and economic costs increase for some countries, governments are under mounting pressure to reopen economies. Some countries, seeing the reemergence of cases, must reintroduce stringent measures. Refocusing on targeted and localized approaches that measure both the value of economic and health considerations is crucial. The costs and benefits of different containment measures should be weighed when making decisions. Policies should be continuously adapted and refined with recent local data, which offer valuable insight into the dynamics of COVID-19.

Establish and communicate clear targets

Setting clear targets helps shape sound policies for the gradual reopening of economies, fosters accountability among governments, and facilitates better coordination among officials and the population. This also makes the public accountable to some degree and helps secure their buy-in, as the achievement of goals and effectiveness of public health interventions are contingent on their behavior and adherence to policies. Finally, clear and transparent target-setting increases the legitimacy of containment measures.

Vaccine procurement and distribution should depend on local data and efficacy

Because risks and immunity levels vary by location, vaccination targets and priorities should be based on local data. In addition, vaccine purchase decisions should depend on the cost of each death averted, efficacy, and price.

Resources

A. Malani. 2020. Forecasting COVID and Vaccination Policy. Presented at ADB's PACER Dialogues. 23 September.

_____. 2020. Tackling Covid-19 through Adaptive Control: Lessons from India. *Apolitical*. 7 August.

A. Malani et al. 2020. Adaptive Control of COVID-19 Outbreaks in India: Local, Gradual, and Trigger-Based Exit Paths from Lockdown. *NBER Working Paper*. No. 27532. Cambridge, Massachusetts: National Bureau of Economic Research.

Enhancing Readiness for Large-Scale Distribution of the COVID-19 Vaccine

Farzana Muhib
Asia Team Lead for Vaccine Implementation, PATH

Hannah Kettler
Director for Financing and Partnerships, PATH's Center for Vaccines Innovation and Access

Huong Vu Minh
Regional Technical Advisor for Vaccine Implementation, PATH

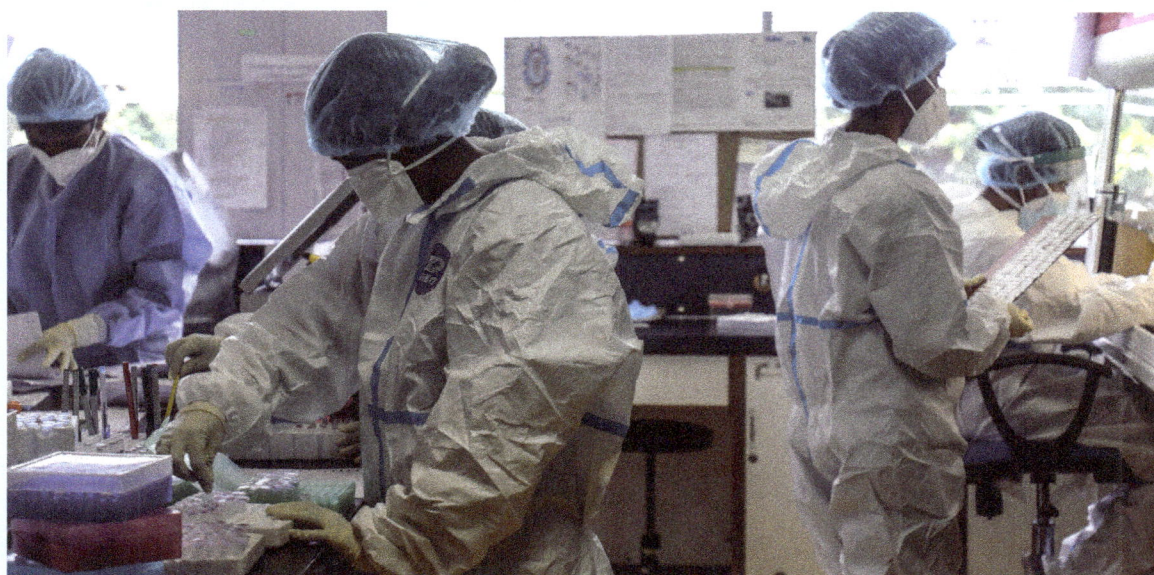

COVID-19 vaccine preparation. When vaccines become available, priority will be given to health workers.

Introduction

The death toll from the coronavirus disease (COVID-19) pandemic and its impact on lives and livelihoods continue to increase as the world waits for more vaccine supply.

Substantial resources have been deployed to accelerate vaccine development. While governments heavily banks on these efforts to return life to normal, a safe and effective vaccine is initially in limited supply. Therefore, a strategy for phased vaccine rollout and continued pandemic control using public health measures and other tools is required.

Countries need to address their unique epidemiologic, demographic, infrastructure, and financing challenges in their national plan for introducing the vaccine in a manner that will reduce mortality, strengthen health system response, and build economic resilience. They also need to work with other countries to ensure equitable and speedy access to the vaccine for all.

High Hopes amid the Challenges

As of 2 February 2021, there were 63 COVID-19 candidate vaccines in clinical evaluation, of which 16 were in Phase 3 trials (requiring 30,000 or more participants), with another 173 candidate vaccines in preclinical evaluation.[11] Four COVID-19 vaccines[12] had submitted data to regulatory authorities for emergency authority use, and the World Health Organization (WHO) is also on track in including vaccines in its Emergency Use Listing with 15 manufacturers undergoing assessment and prequalification.[13] Current vaccine production capacity constraints mean global demand for approved vaccines will far exceed supply for the foreseeable future.

Addressing the epidemiological needs globally requires massive doses for 215 states and territories, but the current best-case estimate is that only 2 billion doses will be available by the end of the year. This shortage obviously raises a conundrum as a study conducted by epidemiologists David Dowdy and Gypsyamber D'Souza suggests that 70% or more of a population would need to be vaccinated to achieve herd immunity. On top of this, some products in the current pipeline will require more than one dose and possibly larger amounts for adults and high-risk groups.

To meet demand, scaling-up vaccine production will be imperative. However, the manufacturing facilities and technology transfer will depend on which vaccine will emerge successful. Another issue lies in the divergence of regulatory requirements and processes across the world, which could be a hurdle for countries to obtain the vaccine quickly. Additionally, the income disparity among countries could result in access inequities. Wealthy economies are well-positioned to directly secure deals with other governments and vaccine developers and to pay more for the much-needed supply—which may leave the low- and middle-income nations at a disadvantage.

Posing another challenge is vaccine delivery—an equally daunting and resource-intensive endeavor as vaccine development. Effectively launching a new vaccine and its efficient delivery will be contingent upon financing and the capacities of health systems, which may be lacking in most low-income countries. Logistical considerations also come into play, with packaging and cold chain requirements conditional on a viable vaccine. The end-to-end temperature control and other storage and handling factors could be major implementation barriers for low-resource nations that likely have inadequate infrastructure. Physical distancing, which is a necessary measure to limit transmission, and vaccine hesitancy could also affect delivery and uptake.

---

[11] World Health Organization (WHO). Draft Landscape of COVID-19 Vaccines (accessed 8 February 2021).

[12] These vaccines are Pfizer-BioNTech, AstraZeneca, Moderna, and Gamaleya as of December 2020.

[13] WHO. Status of COVID-19 Vaccines within WHO EUL/PQ Evaluation Process (20 January 2021).

Obtaining the Vaccine

Funding for vaccines

With the staggering impact of COVID-19 on societies and economies, investments in vaccines must be rapidly mobilized. Along with government contributions, innovative finance mechanisms such as vaccine bonds should be leveraged to fund vaccines. Advance purchase commitments are also useful instruments designed to incentivize vaccine developers to produce enough eligible vaccines through demand guarantees.

Innovative regulatory processes

The crisis urges a rethink of the traditional course of vaccine development to expedite solutions while adhering to high standards of quality, safety, and efficacy. Innovative approaches such as parallel and adaptive trials could speed up testing and comply with safety protocols simultaneously.

Assuming a vaccine is proven safe and efficacious, researchers will apply to regulatory bodies globally for production and distribution. However, the lack of alignment on regulatory standards from one country to another can cause inefficiencies, impeding the immediate introduction of the vaccine across the globe. Therefore, countries need to take steps toward harmonization by coordinating on policies for vaccine approval by regulatory agencies.

Manufacturing scale-up plans

Action should be taken now to build production capacity while R&D is still underway. The facilities and equipment necessary for manufacturing depend on what will turn out to be the best vaccine. Thus, investing in manufacturing at this point could be a risky undertaking. However, there is a strong case for making this uncertain investment given the urgent need for universal access to the vaccine.

The expected high demand for lower-priced vaccines could stimulate local manufacturing, particularly in developing countries, where pharmaceutical or biological manufacturing capacity is in place. In Asia, countries should coordinate to harness the capabilities of neighboring nations with existing facilities.

Countries should evaluate timelines, financial and human resource investment needs, regulatory requirements, and technical risks associated with manufacturing biologics prior to exploring technology transfer options.

Delivering the Vaccine

Planning and communications

Successful vaccine delivery is rooted in proper strategic planning, regular consultations with key stakeholders, prioritization of target segments, review of vaccine suitability, assessment of current delivery channels, and evaluation of resource requirements. Countries need to consider how to introduce the vaccine without disrupting existing routine immunization services.

Advocacy and communications will be an integral part of the vaccine introduction and delivery process, from ensuring the public is informed on the criteria used to allocate doses within the country to reaching target groups not normally part of vaccination programs. Crisis communication plans should also be put in place. Transparency will be essential to mitigate the effects of misinformation and mistrust around vaccines.

Mass campaigns that rely on large gatherings may not be possible or appropriate because of the need for physical distancing. As such, new delivery strategies will likely need to be designed and deployed.

Health systems strengthening

COVID-19 vaccine development, manufacturing, financing, and procurement need to be complemented by strengthening countries' capacity on the development of an allocation methodology, administration of vaccines, reporting, and post-marketing surveillance. Following immunization, post-marketing surveillance will be essential to monitor outcomes rigorously and identify and investigate adverse events in relation to the vaccine.

Delivery costs

In addition to vaccine procurement, the financial implications of distribution should be evaluated. Because COVID-19 requires nontraditional approaches, any additional costs for new modes of distribution should be integrated into national financing plans. The supplies, personal protective equipment, cold chain logistics, among others also need to be factored into the budgeting exercise.

Mobilizing Financing

Governments around the world have marshaled billions of dollars for vaccine R&D in response to COVID-19. Several arrangements between countries and companies have also been established to secure the supply of COVID-19 vaccines. For example, the United States (US) has committed to providing $10 billion to several vaccine developers and vial and syringe manufacturers under Operation Warp Speed.

In July 2020, the International Finance Facility for Immunisation issued over $220 million in vaccine bonds to support the vaccine development efforts of the Coalition for Epidemic Preparedness Innovations (CEPI).

Alongside these initiatives, the Access to COVID-19 Tools Accelerator was formed to serve as a framework for collaboration to make swift progress on the development, production, and equitable access to COVID-19 tests, treatments, and vaccines.

Within the Access to COVID-19 Tools Accelerator, COVID-19 Vaccines Global Access (COVAX) is driving the work on vaccine development, manufacturing, procurement, and delivery at scale, as well as policy and allocation. The Global Alliance for Vaccines and Immunizations (GAVI),[14] CEPI, and the World Health Organization (WHO) lead COVAX. CEPI steers product development and manufacturing capacity efforts, while GAVI manages global financing and procurement in collaboration with WHO to deliver any successful vaccine.

COVAX ensures that the most suitable candidate vaccines get the backing they need to maximize the probability of success. It invites global participation to pool demand and resources to support vaccine procurement. COVAX negotiates 5–10 advance purchase agreements at the highest possible volume and most reasonable price for vaccine candidates that meet the technical threshold criteria. Nine vaccines are part of the COVAX initiative, with an additional nine candidates under evaluation.

To address funding for developing economies, GAVI launched the COVAX Advance Market Commitment (AMC) in June 2020 to support the participation of low-income countries and lower-middle-income countries. Fundraising for COVAX is ongoing to secure $2 billion by the end of 2020 to fund the AMC's initial cost. An additional $3.54 billion will be required to procure 2 billion doses for all COVAX members and $3.2 billion to cover delivery costs by the end of 2021. This leaves a sizable funding gap that will need to be filled. It is also important to note that some potential products are not yet part of COVAX. In terms of supply, the facility will be designating doses for only 20% of the population of participating countries, thereby offering a partial solution to abate the global pandemic.

Given the need for universal coverage and the complexities of vaccine development, procurement, and delivery, countries have been pursuing initiatives apart from COVAX and forging bilateral deals with developers. Inclusive Vaccine Alliance, for instance, has been set up by France, Germany, Italy, and the Netherlands to solidify their negotiating positions and secure doses for the European Union. Bangladesh's Beximco Pharmaceuticals Ltd has entered a pact with Serum Institute of India. Sinovac Biotech in the People's Republic of China has also signed a supply agreement with Bio Farma in Indonesia.

Ensuring Global Access

Through the COVAX Facility, doses will be distributed equitably to participating countries as vaccines become available, giving priority to their health workers and then the most vulnerable segments of their population. Further amounts will be provided based on the country's need, vulnerability, and COVID-19 threats. A small proportion of the total doses may be kept in reserve for emergency and humanitarian response.

Self-financing high-income countries and upper-middle-income countries that are part of COVAX will be required to contribute a portion of the procurement amount up front to support the facility's ability to negotiate supply agreements with companies and a speed premium. About 80 of these countries have submitted nonbinding expressions of interest to COVAX.

Doses for countries with a gross national income per capita under $4,000 or that are eligible for funding under the World Bank's International Development Association will be subsidized through the COVAX AMC. With this facility, the Organisation for Economic Co-operation and Development donors commit to vaccine

---

[14]   It is now called Gavi, the Vaccine Alliance.

manufacturers through official development assistance funds in exchange for sufficient vaccines at a price affordable to these countries. The 92 countries that qualify for AMC include seven Southeast Asian countries: Cambodia, Indonesia, the Lao People's Democratic Republic, Myanmar, the Philippines, Timor-Leste, and Viet Nam.

Expanding Manufacturing Capacity

The estimated supply of 1 billion doses by the end of 2020 is hinged on production expansion. COVAX will encourage manufacturers to invest in scaling-up and help share the associated risks.

Twelve developers in Phase 2/3 trials have announced their vaccine capacity estimates. AstraZeneca and the University of Oxford are projected to have 700 million doses available in 2020, followed by Sinopharm with 200 million and ImmunityBio with 100 million doses.

Recently, GAVI and the Bill & Melinda Gates Foundation announced their collaboration with Serum Institute of India—the world's largest vaccine manufacturer by volume—to accelerate its production and distribution of up to 100 million doses to low-income countries and lower-middle-income countries as part of the COVAX AMC.

Preparing for Vaccine Introduction

To guide countries in ensuring fair allocation of doses for their respective populations, WHO has created a draft framework outlining recommendations on initial doses to health and social workers, then to the elderly and high-risk adults with comorbidities.

As every region and country may be different, vaccination protocols should be reflective of the demographic context. For instance, intergenerational households are common in Asian countries, and the elderly should be given high priority in these locations since they could be at greater risk should younger members of the family return to work and schools.

Moreover, the pandemic severity in countries and their primary objectives—whether it is interrupting transmission, averting deaths and severe cases, or restarting the economy—have implications for shaping their allocation systems and procurement investment plans.

For vaccine candidates and the product attributes that will be most appropriate for delivery in low-income contexts, WHO's Strategic Advisory Group of Experts on Immunization will be issuing recommendations on specific vaccines with their safety and efficacy profiles as well as guidance on delivery approaches as data become available.

For its part, the Asian Development Bank (ADB) supports the strengthening of the health systems of its developing member countries and the regulatory mechanisms of vaccines to facilitate regulatory approval processes of countries and the harmonization of regulatory decisions. ADB is also generating a vaccine knowledge-sharing portal to inform member countries of the latest developments and strengthen their decision-making on future vaccines.

Recommendations

Forge coalitions and partnerships for the common good

Partnerships enable countries to effect innovation, coordinate efforts, and encourage global collaboration. A framework needs to be established for equity in access to prevent supply monopolies. To reduce time lags, countries also need to agree on regulatory policies for vaccine approval through regional cooperation.

Plan for vaccine procurement in tandem with strengthening delivery systems

In this crisis, delays mean more lives are put at risk. Hence, planning for obtaining vaccines should be done in parallel with preparing distribution systems. Countries must identify implementation barriers and bottlenecks, and invest in making improvements to ensure the safe, effective, and efficient rollout of vaccines. These investments will reap long-term gains even after the pandemic.

Use a phased approach for vaccine introduction

With the anticipated scarcity of initial supply, a fair rationing system needs to be established. The first batch of vaccines should be provided in phases to different cohorts—immunizing health-care workers first since they are essential to help preserve the health of others, as well as people at greatest risk of severe illness and death.

When countries apply their allocation framework, these key considerations should be considered: available resources, context, and pandemic stage.

Commit to sharing of data

Facilitating the timely development of safe and quality vaccines and efficient distribution will hinge on data. The exchange of information could advance the pace of vaccine R&D and enable arrangements on the equitable allocation of doses and manufacturing expansion.

After distribution, it will be critical for countries to maintain data-sharing on vaccination outcomes to continuously monitor the vaccine's long-term safety and efficacy.

Build trust and cooperation through transparent communications

Even before the pandemic, vaccine hesitancy has been rising in many parts of the world. Low confidence in vaccines, lack of health literacy, and other concerns about immunization need to be tackled through communication campaigns to cultivate trust and overcome behavioral barriers.

There should also be proactive communication strategies regarding the allocation model criteria, adverse events after immunization, and any new findings on the vaccine.

Leverage innovative financing vehicles

The investments needed to outpace the fast-moving pandemic are immense, and innovative financing instruments can amass large sums of money that no single party could do alone. Mechanisms that crowd in financing could bring the necessary capital to back a diversified portfolio of vaccines and increase the likelihood of finding a viable solution. These could also consolidate demand for a guaranteed market, minimizing risks for manufacturers and encouraging them to supply countries with adequate doses.

Avoid crowding out other vaccines and health services

There is a risk of disruption to routine immunization activities and health services as COVID-19 vaccines are introduced. Countries will need to design strategies to mitigate such risk. If COVID-19 negatively impacts other immunization services, a catch-up program should be initiated for missed vaccinations.

After distributing COVID-19 vaccines, treatment, testing, and contact tracing services should be maintained. Individuals need to be reminded of the importance of upholding standards for COVID-19 infection prevention and control since only a small fraction of the population will be vaccinated in the early stages of the rollout.

Resources

D. Dowdy and G. D'Souza. 2020. *Early Herd Immunity against COVID-19: A Dangerous Misconception*. Johns Hopkins University & Medicine.

International Finance Facility for Immunisation. 2020. IFFIm Issues NOK 2 billion in Vaccine Bonds for COVID-19 Vaccine Development. News release. 7 July.

C. Park et al. 2020. An Updated Assessment of the Economic Impact of COVID-19. *ADB Briefs*. No. 133. Manila.

The New York Times. Coronavirus Vaccine Tracker (accessed 21 March 2021).

PATH. 2020. Enhancing Readiness for Large Scale Vaccine Distribution amid COVID-19. Presented at ADB's PACER Dialogues. 19 August.

World Health Organization (WHO). 2020. 172 Countries and Multiple Candidate Vaccines Engaged in COVID-19 Vaccine Global Access Facility. News release. 24 August.

WHO. 2020. Guiding Principles for Immunization Activities during the COVID-19 Pandemic. Interim guidance. 26 March.

Policy Options to Accelerate Travel and Tourism Recovery in Southeast Asia

Tiffany Misrahi
Vice-President of Policy
World Travel & Tourism Council

Suspended boat operations. The COVID-19 crisis has reduced or suspended operations of travel and tourism businesses, both big and small—from airlines and hotel chains to tour operators and tourist guides.

Introduction

The coronavirus disease (COVID-19) pandemic has undercut travel and tourism demand worldwide. To stem the spread of the virus, the governments closed the borders and businesses, including airlines, restaurants, tourist attractions, and hotels.

Under a baseline scenario where quarantine measures are removed and travel restrictions are eased from June to September 2020, London-based World Travel & Tourism Council (WTTC) sees a $3.4 trillion reduction in the sector's contribution to global GDP and a loss of 121.1 million jobs or about a third of total employment this year. Asia and the Pacific is expected to be the most badly hit region, with lost income of $1.1 trillion and 69.3 million jobs.

The short-, medium-, and long-term impacts on Southeast Asian countries will depend on various factors, including their overall economic strength, the economic importance of travel and tourism, the proportion of domestic to international tourism, and their ability to support the sector through crisis management and recovery efforts.

As demonstrated during previous crises, no stakeholder can drive recovery on its own. Public and private stakeholders need to collaborate and have a coordinated and consistent approach to mitigate impacts and ensure a speedy and effective recovery.

Assessment of Impacts

A demand- and supply-side assessment of COVID-19 impacts on travel and tourism highlights key areas that must be addressed to ensure the swiftest possible recovery.

Demand-side. A mix of economic, psychological, and regulatory effects of the pandemic affects demand. An economic recession will hinder recovery and likely reduce disposable incomes. While certain groups are eagerly awaiting the opportunity to travel again, the pandemic may be increasing risk aversion among certain groups and demographics. In this context, boosting traveler confidence is paramount. Regulations will also influence demand, as the number of visitors allowed to access attractions and services may be reduced. Governments have an important role in stimulating demand and encouraging longer stays per visitor to offset lower demand, and in carefully considering the effects of regulations on business operations.

Supply-side. The travel and tourism value chain is extensive, cutting across industries, including airlines, hotels, cruises, tour operators, digital platforms, geographic distribution systems, restaurants, airports, and car rentals. COVID-19 affects each industry in different ways. How businesses emerge from the crisis will depend on the restrictions they face, the nature and geographic scope of their operations, their demand profile, and their financial health. Currently, nearly all firms have reduced or suspended operations, waiting for lockdowns to ease and travel to resume. Given their typically narrow margins and low cash reserves, bankruptcies and business closures are inevitable unless governments can provide significant and ongoing support by injecting liquidity, providing wage subsidies, and helping businesses manage debt. Importantly, small and medium-sized enterprises (SMEs) comprise about 80% of the sector in Southeast Asia. Homestays, hostels, cafés, and restaurants are often small, family-run enterprises and are particularly vulnerable to lengthy crises. Efforts should focus on supporting SMEs to access affordable credit and temporarily reduce operating costs to avoid mass closures.

Four-Phase Recovery Process

Policies to support travel and tourism recovery may be implemented in four phases.

Phase 1: Managing and Mitigating the Crisis

Policy options for immediate sector support and implementation

1. **Protect workers' livelihoods.** Provide financial assistance to safeguard workers' incomes and support skills training.
2. **Fiscal support.** Waive taxes, fees, and other government charges for 1 year or longer.
3. **Inject liquidity and cash flow.** Provide cash flow assistance to support large and small businesses, as well as targeted support to severely affected, structurally important subsectors. Consider extending vital, appropriately sized interest-free loans to companies and SMEs to prevent their collapse.
4. **Support the informal sector, including business registration.** Promote business registration to broaden and make more effective support from government and financial lending institutions.
5. **Comply with travel bans.** Implement measures that support directives protecting public health.

Phase 2: Restarting the Travel and Tourism Sector

Policy options to enable successful resumption of services

1. **Coordinate subsectors.** Ensure coordinated, holistic approaches to restarting different subsectors (e.g., food services, conventions, and exhibitions). Enable coordination between and among governments to manage phased reopening to different markets.
2. **Define new global protocols.** Implement health and safety protocols across subsectors to rebuild confidence among consumers, assuring safe travel once restrictions are lifted.
3. **Regulatory relief and reinvestment.** Implement moratoriums on penalties linked to the drop in tourism. Reinvest tourism-specific taxes to protect public goods that are important for tourism and increase public financing for travel and tourism projects that upgrade public facilities and services.
4. **Metrics and strategy.** Establish metrics to measure and manage the rate, extent, and length of recovery. Establish timely data-driven plans and criteria on how and when to reopen borders in a safe, timely, and coordinated manner. Use this information to deliver evidence-based communication that inspires travelers' confidence.
5. **Prioritize the sector.** Continue to prioritize private sector liquidity needs through explicit political and financial support.
6. **Ease travel restrictions.** Ensure that any travel restrictions are managed adaptively and remain proportionate to public health threats.
7. **Build sustainability.** Foster public–private–community dialogue to build consensus on delivering shared objectives better to boost sustainability.

Phase 3: Reaching Recovery

Policies to rebuild traveler confidence, inspire wanderlust, and strengthen the enabling environment

1. **Lead with domestic travel.** Promote domestic travel, recognizing it is likely to start sooner and more quickly than international travel.

2. **Reinspire wanderlust while providing reassurance and rebuilding traveler confidence.** Communicate proactively and facilitate travel and design promotions to reinspire wanderlust. Consider policies that enable appropriate pricing, packaging, and flexible reservations and cancellations. Provide travelers reassurance through better visibility of health and safety protocols and offer simple, reliable, and guaranteed travel insurance to ensure that travelers feel safe.

3. **Facilitate recovery through supportive regulation and incentives.** Ensure that any necessary regulatory actions facilitate long-term recovery and support.

Phase 4: Redesigning the "New Normal"

Policies for a later stage when domestic and international travel approach precrisis levels and the travel and tourism sector has successfully adapted to shifting expectations and requirements

1. **Determine new requirements and expectations.** Use data and research to understand shifting trends, expectations, and requirements of different travel segments.

2. **Collaborate to develop policies that shape the new normal.** Ensure that all sector actors are involved in the definition and implementation of new policies and regulations that influence the sector.

3. **Embrace new technologies.** Promote technologies such as biometrics and digital platforms that enable a safe and seamless journey.

4. **Communicate openly, promoting domestic and international travel to revitalize the sector.** Trust is a key currency; hence, all stakeholders will demand policies that require transparent communication and respect for privacy, particularly digital identities.

Key Considerations

Travel and tourism can and should be part of the solution to drive overall economic recovery, but this requires governments to recognize the sector's value and develop coordinated supportive policies and messages. Indeed, the scale and nature of the COVID-19 crisis are such that central governments must take a leading role in coordinating the recovery from within and across borders. The private sector has a key role in driving the recovery, but this must be done according to clear guidelines and communication from governments, who themselves can take guidance from relevant industry associations and international organizations.

The governments should take the following three key considerations as they lead the recovery.

1. **Supportive regulation**

   Any necessary regulatory actions should facilitate recovery, increase resilience, and ensure a healthier travel and tourism sector in the longer term.

   As countries recover from the pandemic, hard-hit governments are likely to face the temptation to capture new revenues just as equally hard-hit companies are starting to reopen and regain footing. As such, governments will need to find a balance between generating public funds and enabling the sector to drive growth and generate jobs. Health and safety regulations, such as arrival quarantines, will need to be managed carefully to avoid dissuading visitors.

   Governments can consider creating incentives to support SMEs and putting tourism infrastructure investment on the fast track. Members of the Association of Southeast Asian Nations (ASEAN) should continue to support open skies policies, including pushing forward with the European Union–ASEAN and the ASEAN Open Skies Agreement as appropriate, while reviewing the use of air space and routes to reduce fuel costs and carbon dioxide emissions.

2. **Effective coordination**

   Governments should ensure that stakeholders are broadly involved in defining and implementing new policies and regulations relating to the sector. Each policy recommendation listed above will require different players to be involved, including ministries (e.g., health, transport, finance, and interior), government agencies, state-owned enterprises, private sector, and relevant international organizations and industry associations.

   Joint public–private approaches at the national and international levels will be critical to reestablish effective operations, remove travel barriers, reopen borders, and ensure the efficient resumption of flights, movement of people, and widescale travel that is essential to rebuild confidence in the sector.

   It will also be important for governments to work with the private sector and health experts to define global protocols for the new normal. These protocols should be grounded in science and easily adopted worldwide by businesses of every size across all travel subsectors.

   Similarly, a wide range of ministries, travel, and tourism actors and technology providers will need to work together for destinations to provide a safe and seamless travel experience, combining the latest technology and protocols to increase health and hygiene standards.

   In a post-COVID-19 world, the use of biometrics, loyalty rewards, credit cards, and travel history, proof of immunity or vaccine, and other personal information will be essential to allow governments and travel providers to more efficiently and safely move the traveler throughout the journey. This is especially relevant to streamline requirements for travelers to present and verify their identity, travel history (recently visited countries), and medical history (i.e., vaccinations) at multiple touchpoints.

Key factors for success require extensive collaboration at the national and international levels. These factors include

- interoperability (scalable solutions with seamless public and private sector interaction);

- secure data collection and transparent data sharing using minimal personal information and data privacy; and

- intergovernmental and private sector cooperation (bilateral data-sharing agreements between multiple governments and between the public and private sectors).

3. **People-centric approaches**

Given the nature of travel and tourism, recovery initiatives also need to be people-centric, focusing on how to safeguard residents, tourists, and employees equally. As such, identifying and engaging with these stakeholder groups is critical to effectively disseminate information, provide reassurances, and share best-practice approaches.

Initial Outcomes

Most economies are still somewhere between Phases 1 and 2 of managing and mitigating the crisis and carefully restarting the sector. As such, it is still too early to measure the success of most recovery initiatives. However, Phase 1 shows various examples of how economies have swiftly implemented travel and tourism support measures.

1. **Worker protection**

France is implementing one of the most generous furlough schemes, covering 12.2 million workers and costing €26 billion ($31 billion). It pays 70% of workers' gross salary (or about 84% of the net salary), up to €6,927 ($8,387) gross per month. Minimum wage employees receive 100% compensation.

Singapore has rolled out a $5 billion Jobs Support Scheme that co-funds the first S$4,600 ($3,463) of gross monthly wages. There are three tiers of co-funding, with tourism and aviation in the highest tier at 75%. The subsequent tiers are co-funded at 50% and 25%.

2. **Liquidity measures**

In the **United Kingdom**, destination management organizations benefit from a £1.3 million ($1.8 million) wage support scheme. They can receive up to £2,500 ($3,468) per month for two non-furloughed staff and up to £5,000 ($6,933) to cover operating costs.

The United Kingdom also introduced a £25,000 ($34,680) business grant scheme for businesses in the retail, hospitality, tourism, and leisure sectors. The scheme is open to businesses that occupy rental properties as sole tenants.

Hong Kong, China is a bolstering capacity for tourism promotion. In February 2020, it allocated an additional $90.2 million for its tourism board to bolster external promotion.

Portugal has extended a €200 million ($241 million) credit line for travel agencies, animation, and events; €900 million ($1 billion) for hotels; and €60 million ($72 million) for micro-companies operating in the tourism sector. Portugal's National Tourism Authority manages the program.

Denmark established the Danish Travel Guarantee Fund, which compensates consumers facing cancellations resulting from bankrupt travel organizers. It provided a state loan facility of $225 million to the fund.

To prevent liquidity crises in cruise lines, **Finland**, **France**, **Germany**, **Italy**, and **Norway** agreed on procedures to allow cruise lines to suspend repayments (1 year) for cruise ships financed with state export credit guarantees.

3. **Fiscal measures**

The **Russian Federation** is implementing tax and social security contribution holidays for companies in tourism and aviation. **Indonesia** suspended the 10% hotel and restaurant local tax for 6 months. **Malaysia** suspended tax installments by 6 months for tourism businesses. The **United Kingdom** waived retail, leisure, and tourism business property taxes for 12 months.

Other initiatives related to the phased approach highlighted in this policy brief involve sustainable infrastructure investment, domestic tourism, and coordination.

Iceland launched a $110 million investment acceleration initiative with several projects supporting travel and tourism, such as public infrastructure and greenspace improvements, technology development, and electrification of rental vehicles.

Viet Nam's tourism promotion campaign "Vietnamese People Travel in Viet Nam" debuted in mid-May 2020 to introduce quality tourism products and service packages at reasonable prices. Similar efforts followed in Thailand, Indonesia, and the Philippines, as they eased domestic travel restrictions.

Sri Lanka released comprehensive guidelines for a limited resumption of international tourism from 8 June 2020 in line with the Ministry of Health and the World Health Organization (WHO). The Sri Lanka Tourism Development Authority will implement the guidelines with the cooperation, support, and involvement of relevant public and private bodies and other development partners. Sri Lanka has synthesized the information in a clear, user-friendly Q&A format.

Governments and other stakeholders must monitor the impact of their various recovery initiatives to learn from experience and be better prepared for any future shocks.

Recommendations

World Travel & Tourism Council (WTTC) recommends that governments and the private sector adopt a risk-based approach based on high- and low-risk contexts and adopt policy measures accordingly. There is no one-size-fits-all solution. The health and safety of both travelers and those working within the sector are paramount, but this must be carefully balanced with the socioeconomic implications of the measures taken.

WTTC foresees three possible outcomes for the global travel and tourism sector:

1. **Downside scenario.** Easing of current restrictions from September for short-haul and regional travel, from October for mid-haul, and from November for the long-haul. This scenario may result in 197.5 million jobs lost in the travel and tourism sector and a loss of $5,543 billion in global GDP. Meanwhile, visitor numbers may drop by 73% for international arrivals.

2. **Baseline scenario.** Easing of restrictions from June for regional travel, from July for short-haul or regional travel, from August for mid-haul, and from September for the long-haul. This scenario may result in 121.1 million jobs lost and a loss of $3,435 billion. Visitor numbers may drop by 53% for international arrivals and 34% for domestic arrivals.

3. **Upside scenario.** Easing of current measures from June for short-haul and regional travel, from July for mid-haul, and from August for the long-haul. This scenario may result in 98.2 million jobs lost, half the number in the worst-case scenario, and a loss of $2,686 billion. Meanwhile, visitor numbers may drop by 41% for international arrivals and 26% for domestic arrivals.

While the best-case scenario will still result in a devastating blow for travel and tourism, this outcome avoids additional harm to the sector as a result of prolonged travel restrictions and protects almost 100 million jobs around the world. This scenario can still be achieved by the global travel and tourism sector if governments implement WTTC's recommended phased policy actions and steps below.

Firstly, the immediate removal and replacement of any quarantine measures, with "air corridors" to countries with similar circumstances to stimulate the travel and tourism sector and the global economy, as well as the removal of travel advisories and bans on nonessential international travel, which prevent insurance protection cover for travelers.

Secondly, the adoption of global health and safety protocols, such as the "Safe Travels" initiative recently launched by WTTC, to assure travelers that enhanced health and hygiene measures are in place and that it is safe to travel again.

Thirdly, the implementation of rapid test and trace strategies to help contain the spread of the virus while still allowing people to travel responsibly at home and abroad.

And finally, greater and sustained collaboration between the public and private sectors to ensure a coordinated global approach to the crisis.

Resources

World Travel & Tourism Council (WTTC). Economic Impact Reports (accessed 1 July 2021).

WTTC. 'Safe Travels': Global Protocols & Stamp for the New Normal.

_____. 2019. Crisis Preparedness, Management & Recovery.

_____. 2020. More than 197M Travel & Tourism Jobs Will Be Lost Due to Prolonged Travel Restrictions, According to New Research from WTTC. News. 10 June.

_____. 2020. Seamless Traveller Journey: WTTC Discussion Paper: Data Facilitation—Privacy Perspective.

_____. 2020. Tourism Response and Recovery: Rebuilding Economic & Social Benefits; Reinspiring Traveler Confidence. Presented at ADB's PACER Dialogues. 24 June.

_____. 2021. Government COVID-19 Policies. 18 February.

About the PACER Dialogues

Policy Actions for COVID-19 Economic Recovery (PACER) Dialogues, supported by the Asian Development Bank (ADB) under the "Brunei Darussalam–Indonesia–Malaysia–Philippines East ASEAN Growth Area (BIMP-EAGA), Indonesia–Malaysia–Thailand Growth Triangle (IMT-GT), and Greater Mekong Subregion (GMS) Capacity Building Program, or B-I-G Program, explored measures that can help B-I-G member countries, Singapore, and Timor-Leste bounce back from the coronavirus disease (COVID-19) pandemic and accelerate economic recovery.

Overcoming COVID-19 Together

At a Special ASEAN Summit on COVID-19 on 14 April 2020, leaders called on the Association of Southeast Asian Nations (ASEAN) to "act jointly and decisively to control the spread of the disease while mitigating its adverse impact on our people's livelihood, our societies, and economies." Leaders also called for sharing best practices between member states and external partners to respond to COVID-19 effectively. Consistent with this call for action, the B-I-G Program convened the PACER Dialogues to share cutting-edge knowledge and best practices, and explore means of strengthening cooperation to mitigate the devastating effects of COVID-19.

Sharing Approaches and Lessons to Accelerate COVID-19 Recovery

Countries in the region and across the world are grappling with balancing policy responses that can mitigate the economic costs of the COVID-19 crisis while also minimizing risks to society. The PACER Dialogues shared global, regional, and country-level good practices and lessons that can provide new ideas and actionable insights for countries as they lay the groundwork for medium-term economic recovery. Sharing knowledge and learning from others allowed countries to explore a broader range of policy options as they tailor recovery measures to the unique context of their respective nations.

Objectives

PACER Dialogues objectives included

- enhancing awareness on policy issues and actions that can facilitate economic recovery;
- sharing knowledge, lessons, and experiences on COVID-19 recovery strategies, policies, and plans;
- exploring collaborative responses and coordinated actions geared toward increased resilience, preparedness, and effective recovery; and
- strengthening connections between policy makers, development planners, and relevant stakeholders tasked with spearheading the COVID-19 crisis recovery.

Format, Process, and Policy Briefs

A series of 90-minute PACER Dialogues were held between June and September 2020. The dialogue process included (i) moderators' introduction, (ii) experts' presentation, (iii) reactions from panel discussants, (iv) open discussion with questions and inputs by participating government officials, and (v) moderator synthesis or summary.

The PACER Dialogues were provided to help decision makers broaden their perspectives, appreciate the wider implications of critical policy choices, and identify concrete policy actions. Background papers were provided in advance to facilitate informed discussions. Policy briefs for each dialogue were produced as knowledge products (outputs) and shared on ADB's knowledge platform, Development Asia.

Themes and Topics

Topics of the PACER Dialogues had three main categories: (i) overarching strategic approaches for forging national strategies for COVID-19 economic recovery, (ii) cross-cutting thematic and sector-specific approaches to facilitate economic recovery and mitigate the devastating effects of COVID-19, and (iii) regional cooperation responses to COVID-19 to complement national strategies.

- Overarching strategic approaches for national recovery included economic and financial measures to tackle COVID-19; good practices in designing, financing, and implementing plans for bouncing back from COVID-19; employing big data and digital technology to enhance COVID-19 responses; and mobilizing finance in the wake of COVID-19.

- Cross-cutting thematic and sector approaches included health measures to enhance resilience to pandemics, interventions for economic reopenings, and readiness for vaccine distribution; supporting small and medium-sized enterprises (SMEs) and start-ups to mitigate the negative effects of the crisis; developing effective social protection responses; helping the tourism industry bounce back from COVID-19; and harnessing digital technology for education.

- Regional cooperation responses to complement national strategies and emphasize public goods were also explored, such as multisector interventions in health, tourism, and migration.

Experts

Select ADB staff, government officials, academicians, private sector experts, and development partners were invited to serve as presenters and discussants.

Participants and Audience

Policy makers and planners involved in the various policy domains of the COVID-19 crisis recovery, especially from the ministries of finance and the BIMP-EAGA, IMT-GT, and GMS national secretariats, served as core participants. Depending on the themes and topics, participation was extended to other ministries, the private sector, academe, civil society, and international organizations.

A total of 738 participants from ASEAN member countries, the People's Republic of China, and Timor-Leste, including representatives from development partners, attended the 12 PACER Dialogues—566 participants were government officials from BIMP-EAGA, IMT-GT, and GMS with 231 (41%) women, and the majority (418, 74%) were at the director level and above.

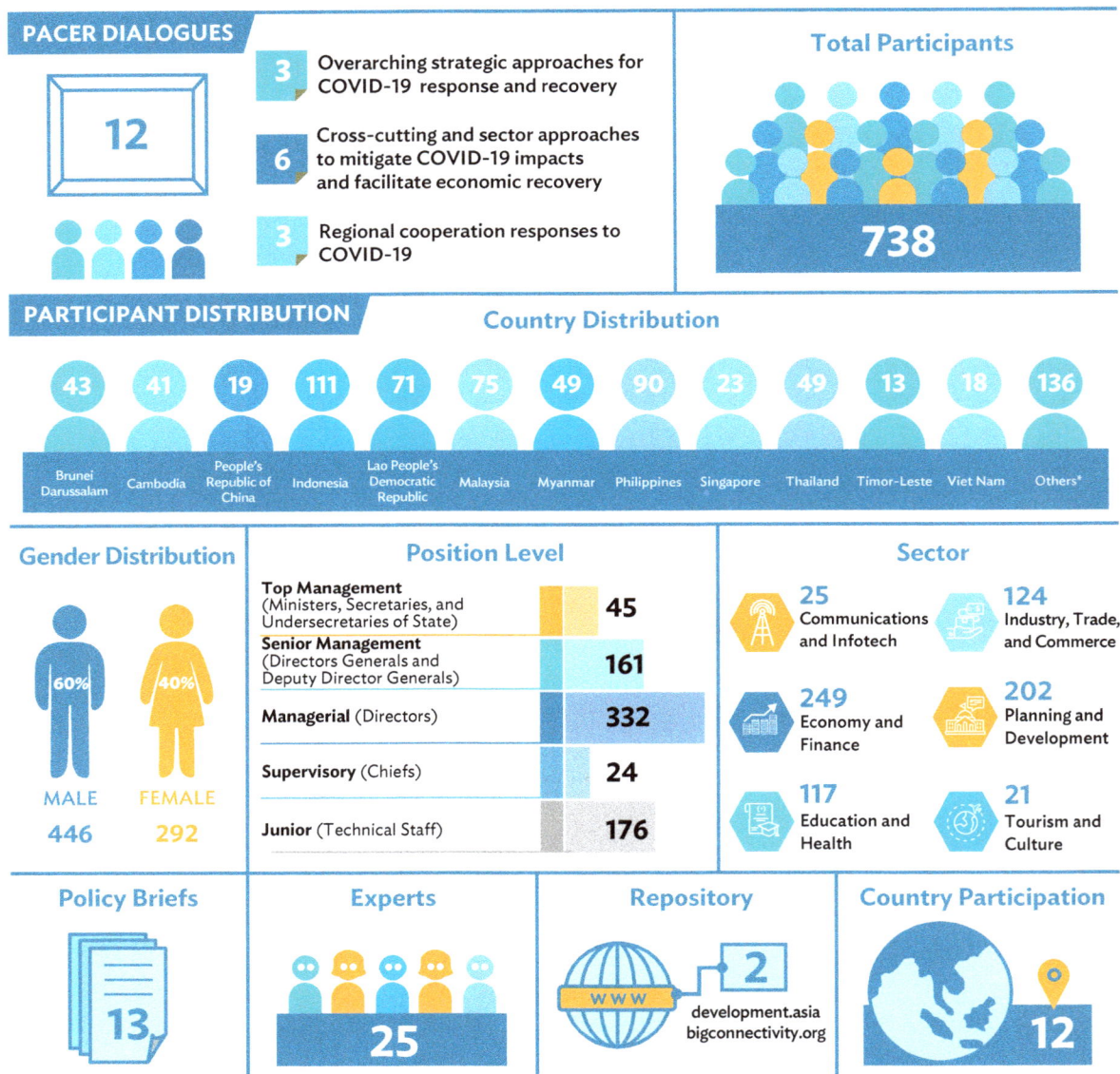

PACER DIALOGUES

12

- **3** Overarching strategic approaches for COVID-19 response and recovery
- **6** Cross-cutting and sector approaches to mitigate COVID-19 impacts and facilitate economic recovery
- **3** Regional cooperation responses to COVID-19

Total Participants

738

PARTICIPANT DISTRIBUTION

Country Distribution

Brunei Darussalam	Cambodia	People's Republic of China	Indonesia	Lao People's Democratic Republic	Malaysia	Myanmar	Philippines	Singapore	Thailand	Timor-Leste	Viet Nam	Others*
43	41	19	111	71	75	49	90	23	49	13	18	136

Gender Distribution

MALE **446** (60%)
FEMALE **292** (40%)

Position Level

Top Management (Ministers, Secretaries, and Undersecretaries of State)	45
Senior Management (Directors Generals and Deputy Director Generals)	161
Managerial (Directors)	332
Supervisory (Chiefs)	24
Junior (Technical Staff)	176

Sector

- **25** Communications and Infotech
- **124** Industry, Trade, and Commerce
- **249** Economy and Finance
- **202** Planning and Development
- **117** Education and Health
- **21** Tourism and Culture

Policy Briefs
13

Experts
25

Repository
2
www
development.asia
bigconnectivity.org

Country Participation
12

*representatives from private sector and nonprofit organizations, ADB, and development partners.
Source: ADB.

Invitation, Dissemination, and Repository

The policy dialogues were by invitation and coursed through the BIMP-EAGA and IMT-GT senior officials, GMS national coordinators, and ministries of finance. Background papers were provided in advance to facilitate informed discussions. A public repository summarizing PACER Dialogues (without attribution) was hosted on ADB's knowledge platform, Development Asia.

List of 2020 PACER Dialogues

No.	Date	Title or Theme	Experts	Policy Brief/s
1	3 June	Tackling COVID-19: Economic and Financial Measures of the Republic of Korea	• Kwangchul Ji Director of International Financial Institutions Division, Ministry of Economy and Finance, Republic of Korea	• Policy Lessons from a Pandemic: The Korean Experience
2	17 June	Experience and Lessons of New Zealand in Responding to COVID-19	• Mark Blackmore Senior Representative for Singapore, India, and Southeast Asia, New Zealand Treasury • Mario Di Maio Principal Advisor, New Zealand Treasury	• Lessons We Can Learn from New Zealand's COVID-19 Strategy
3	24 June	Tourism: Respond, Restart, and Recover	• Tiffany Misrahi Vice President of Policy, World Travel & Tourism Council • Mario Hardy Chief Executive Officer, Pacific Asia Travel Association • Jens Thraenhart Executive Director, Mekong Tourism Coordinating Office	• Policy Options to Accelerate Travel and Tourism Recovery in Southeast Asia
4	1 July	Minimum Public Health Interventions for Post COVID-19 Lockdown: Lives and Livelihoods	• Jeremy Lim Co-Director of Global Health, Saw Swee Hock School of Public Health, National University of Singapore	• Harmonizing Health Standards for Post-Quarantine COVID-19 Settings
5	8 July	Bouncing Back Support to SMEs for COVID-19 Recovery	• Paul Vandenberg Senior Economist, Economic Research and Regional Cooperation Department, Asian Development Bank • Foo Ngee Kee Co-Founder and President of the SME Association of Sabah	• How SMEs Can Bounce Back from the COVID-19 Crisis

continued on the next page

Continued

6	15 July	Migration and Health: Implications of COVID-19 and Achieving Universal Health Coverage	• Patrick Duigan Regional Migration Health Advisor for Asia and the Pacific, International Organization for Migration • Jadej Thammatcharee Deputy Secretary-General, National Health Security Office, Thailand • Heather Canon Vice President for Capacity Building, ELEVATE	• Coming Out Stronger from COVID-19: Policy Options on Migrant Health and Immigration
7	22 July	Harnessing Digital Technologies for Education amid COVID-19	• Ashish Dhawan Founder and Chairman, Central Square Foundation • Chad Pasha Head of Asia Pacific for Global Government Partnerships, Coursera	• An Equity-Focused Digital Strategy for Education during and after COVID-19 • Policy Lessons from Coursera: Mitigating Education Disruptions and Job Loss
8	4 August	Post-COVID-19 New Normal: Implications for Startup Ecosystems	• Stephan Kuester Head, Global Ecosystem Strategy, Startup Genome • Seow Hui Lim Director, Startup Development, Innovation and Enterprise Group, Enterprise Singapore • Christiaan Kaptein Partner, Integra Partners	• Fostering Resilient Startup Ecosystems in the New Normal
9	12 August	Accelerating Digital Financial Services and Infrastructure	• David Lee Kuo Chuen Professor, Singapore University of Social Sciences • Haerok Ko General Manager, Korea Financial Telecommunications and Clearings Institute	• Building the Infrastructure for Digital Finance during COVID-19 and Beyond
10	19 August	Enhancing Readiness for Large-Scale Vaccine Distribution amid COVID-19	• Farzana Muhib Asia Team Lead for Vaccine Implementation, PATH • Hannah Kettler Director for Financing and Partnerships, PATH's Center for Vaccines Innovation and Access • Huong Minh Vu Regional Technical Advisor for Vaccine Implementation, PATH	• Enhancing Readiness for Large-Scale Distribution of the COVID-19 Vaccine
11	26 August	Social Protection Interventions as Medium- and Long-Term Responses amid COVID-19 and Beyond	• Valentina Barca Independent Social Protection Expert • Edward Archibald Independent Social Protection Expert	• Social Protection Interventions as Medium- and Long-Term Responses to the Pandemic
12	23 September	Adaptive Control of COVID-19 Outbreaks: Policy Approaches	• Anup Malani Professor, University of Chicago	• Adaptive Control of COVID-19 Outbreaks: Policy Approaches

COVID-19 = coronavirus disease, PACER = Policy Actions for COVID-19 Economic Recovery, SMEs = small and medium-sized enterprises.
Source: ADB.

About the B-I-G Program

The Brunei Darussalam–Indonesia–Malaysia–Philippines East ASEAN Growth Area (BIMP-EAGA), the Indonesia–Malaysia–Thailand Growth Triangle (IMT-GT), and the Greater Mekong Subregion (GMS) Capacity Building Program, or B-I-G Program, is a regional capacity development initiative for government officials to enhance capacities in developing policies, programs, and projects that support physical, institutional, and people-to-people connectivity in Southeast Asia and the People's Republic of China. The B-I-G Program provides opportunities for knowledge and experience sharing and networking among the three subregional programs, given their unique roles as building blocks for Asian integration. It is funded by the Asian Development Bank (ADB) and the governments of the Republic of Korea and the People's Republic of China.

B-I-G Program Team

ALFREDO PERDIGUERO
Director, Regional Cooperation and Operations
Coordination Division, Southeast Asia Department
Asian Development Bank

JASON RUSH
Principal Operations Communications Specialist

MARIA THERESA A. BUGAYONG
Operations Officer (Resource Planning)

PAMELA ASIS-LAYUGAN
Institutional and Capacity Development
Specialist (Consultant)

JORDANA QUEDDENG-COSME
Regional Development Analyst (Consultant)

ALONA MAE H. AGUSTIN
Regional Development Analyst (Consultant)

6 ADB Avenue, Mandaluyong City
1550 Metro Manila, Philippines
www.bigconnectivity.org